THE NEW
Art and Science
OF TEACHING

Mathematics

NATHAN D. LANG-RAAD   ROBERT J. MARZANO

A joint publication

ASCD   Solution Tree

555 North Morton Street
Bloomington, IN 47404
800.733.6786 (toll free) / 812.336.7700
FAX: 812.336.7790

email: info@SolutionTree.com
SolutionTree.com

Visit **go.SolutionTree.com/instruction** to download the free reproducibles in this book.

Printed in the United States of America

Library of Congress Cataloging-in-Publication Data

Names: Lang, Nathan D., author. | Marzano, Robert J., author.
Title: The new art and science of teaching mathematics / Nathan D. Lang-Raad
   and Robert J. Marzano.
Description: Bloomington, IN : Solution Tree Press, [2019] | Includes
   bibliographical references and index.
Identifiers: LCCN 2018042848 | ISBN 9781945349652 (perfect bound)
Subjects: LCSH: Mathematics--Study and teaching. | Mathematics
   teachers--Training of. | Effective teaching. | Teaching--Aids and devices.
   | Learning, Psychology of.
Classification: LCC QA11.2 .L342 2019 | DDC 510.71--dc23 LC record available at https://lccn.loc.gov/2018042848

Solution Tree
Jeffrey C. Jones, CEO
Edmund M. Ackerman, President

Solution Tree Press
President and Publisher: Douglas M. Rife
Associate Publisher: Sarah Payne-Mills
Art Director: Rian Anderson
Managing Production Editor: Kendra Slayton
Senior Production Editor: Suzanne Kraszewski
Senior Editor: Amy Rubenstein
Copy Editor: Miranda Addonizio
Proofreader: Elisabeth Abrams
Text and Cover Designer: Rian Anderson
Editorial Assistant: Sarah Ludwig

I dedicate this book to my husband, Herbie Raad. Your unending support, encouragement, creativity, and love inspires me to aim higher than I ever could have on my own. You kept me on schedule, edited and proofed, and gave me the best advice. Thank you for being you. I love you so.

—Nathan Lang-Raad

Visit **go.SolutionTree.com/instruction** to download the free reproducibles in this book.

Table of Contents

About the Authors

Nathan D. Lang-Raad, EdD, is a speaker, author, and professional learning facilitator. He is chief education officer at WeVideo. Throughout his career, he has served as a teacher, assistant principal, university adjunct professor, consultant, and education strategist. He was director of elementary curriculum and instruction for Metropolitan Nashville Public Schools, as well as education supervisor at NASA's Johnson Space Center. He speaks at both local and national professional conferences, and is the cofounder of Bammy Award–nominated #LeadUpChat, an educational leadership professional learning network (PLN) on Twitter. Nathan is also the cofounder of #divergED, a Twitter chat focused on divergent thinking and innovations in education. He is a Google Certified Educator, Microsoft Innovative Educator, and 2016 Apple Teacher. He serves on the Children's Right to Read International Literacy Association Task Force and is a board member on the Student Voice Foundation.

Nathan has written several blog posts that have been featured on the EdTech K–12, Corwin Connect, Education Week, K–12 Blueprint, and Solution Tree websites.

Nathan received a bachelor of arts degree in general science–chemistry from Harding University in Searcy, Arkansas, a master of education degree in administration and supervision from the University of Houston–Victoria, and a doctorate of education degree in learning organizations and strategic change from David Lipscomb University in Nashville, Tennessee.

To learn more about Nathan's work, visit www.drlangraad.com or follow @drlangraad on Twitter.

Robert J. Marzano, PhD, is the cofounder and chief academic officer of Marzano Research in Denver, Colorado. During his fifty years in the field of education, he has worked with educators as a speaker and trainer and has authored more than forty books and three hundred articles on topics such as instruction, assessment, writing and implementing standards, cognition, effective leadership, and school intervention. His books include *The Art and Science of Teaching*, *The Handbook for the New Art and Science of Teaching*, *The New Art and Science of Teaching Writing*, *The New Art and Science of Teaching Reading*, *The New Art and Science of Classroom Assessment*, *Leaders of Learning*, *The Classroom Strategies Series*, *A Handbook for High Reliability Schools*, *Awaken the Learner*, and *Managing the Inner World of Teaching*.

His practical translations of the most current research and theory into classroom strategies are known internationally and are widely practiced by both teachers and administrators.

He received a bachelor's degree from Iona College in New York, a master's degree from Seattle University, and a doctorate from the University of Washington.

To learn more about Dr. Marzano's work, visit www.marzanoresearch.com.

Introduction

The New Art and Science of Teaching (Marzano, 2017) is a comprehensive model of instruction with a rather long developmental lineage. Specifically, four books spanning two decades precede and inform *The New Art and Science of Teaching* and its use in the field.

1. *Classroom Instruction That Works: Research-Based Strategies for Increasing Student Achievement* (Marzano, Pickering, & Pollock, 2001)
2. *Classroom Management That Works: Research-Based Strategies for Every Teacher* (Marzano, Marzano, & Pickering, 2003)
3. *Classroom Assessment and Grading That Work* (Marzano, 2006)
4. *The Art and Science of Teaching: A Comprehensive Framework for Effective Instruction* (Marzano, 2007)

The first three books address specific components of the teaching process, namely instruction, management, and assessment. The final book puts all three components together into a comprehensive model of teaching. It also makes a strong case for the fact that research (in other words, science) must certainly guide good teaching, but teachers must also develop good teaching as art. Even if they use precisely the same instructional strategies, two highly effective teachers will have shaped and adapted those strategies to adhere to their specific personalities, the subject matter they teach, and their students' unique needs. Stated differently, we can never accurately articulate effective teaching as a set of strategies that all teachers must execute in precisely the same way.

The comprehensive model in the book *The New Art and Science of Teaching* (Marzano, 2017) reflects a greatly expanded and updated version of *The Art and Science of Teaching* (Marzano, 2007). One of the unique aspects of *The New Art and Science of Teaching* is that it focuses on student learning, rather than being teacher focused, as we depict in figure I.1:

Source: Marzano, 2017, p. 5.

Figure I.1: The teaching and learning progression.

According to figure I.1, the intervening variables between effectively applying an instructional strategy and enhanced student learning are specific mental states and processes in the minds of learners. If teachers do not produce these mental states and processes as a result of employing a given strategy, then that strategy will have little or no effect on students. This implies that teachers should heighten their level of awareness as they use instructional strategies for maximum efficacy.

The Overall Model

At a basic level, the model in *The New Art and Science of Teaching* (Marzano, 2017) is a framework that educators can use to organize the majority (if not all) of the instructional strategies that research and theory identify. The model has several parts: three overarching categories, ten design areas, and forty-three specific elements.

Three Categories

At the highest level of organization, the model has three overarching categories.

1. *Feedback* refers to the all-important information loop teachers must establish with students so that students know what they should be learning about specific topics and their current level of performance on these topics.
2. *Content* refers to the sequencing and pacing of lessons such that students move smoothly from initial understanding to applying knowledge in new and creative ways.
3. *Context* refers to those strategies that ensure all students meet these psychological needs: engagement, order, a sense of belonging, and high expectations.

Embedded in these three overarching categories are more specific categories of teacher actions (design areas).

Ten Design Areas

In *The New Art and Science of Teaching* framework, each of the ten design areas is associated with a specific teacher action, as follows.

1. Providing and communicating clear learning goals
2. Using assessments
3. Conducting direct instruction lessons
4. Conducting practicing and deepening lessons
5. Conducting knowledge application lessons
6. Using strategies that appear in all types of lessons
7. Using engagement strategies
8. Implementing rules and procedures
9. Building relationships
10. Communicating high expectations

Table I.1 shows the ten teacher actions within the three categories and describes the desired student mental states and processes for each. For example, when the teacher conducts a direct instruction lesson (the third design area), the goal is that students will understand which parts of the content are important and how they fit together.

Table I.1: Teacher Actions and Student Mental States and Processes

	Teacher Actions	Student Mental States and Processes
Feedback	Providing and Communicating Clear Learning Goals	1. Students understand the progression of knowledge they are expected to master and where they are along that progression.
	Using Assessments	2. Students understand how test scores and grades relate to their status on the progression of knowledge they are expected to master.
Content	Conducting Direct Instruction Lessons	3. When content is new, students understand which parts are important and how the parts fit together.
	Conducting Practicing and Deepening Lessons	4. After teachers present new content, students deepen their understanding and develop fluency in skills and processes.
	Conducting Knowledge Application Lessons	5. After teachers present new content, students generate and defend claims through knowledge application tasks.
	Using Strategies That Appear in All Types of Lessons	6. Students continually integrate new knowledge with old knowledge and revise their understanding accordingly.
Context	Using Engagement Strategies	7. Students are paying attention, energized, intrigued, and inspired.
	Implementing Rules and Procedures	8. Students understand and follow rules and procedures.
	Building Relationships	9. Students feel welcome, accepted, and valued.
	Communicating High Expectations	10. Typically reluctant students feel valued and do not hesitate to interact with the teacher or their peers.

Each of the ten design areas corresponds with a *design question*. These questions help teachers plan units and lessons within those units. Table I.2 shows the design questions that correspond with each design area.

Table I.2: Design Questions

	Design Areas	Design Questions
Feedback	1. Providing and Communicating Clear Learning Goals	How will I communicate clear learning goals that help students understand the progression of knowledge they are expected to master and where they are along that progression?
	2. Using Assessments	How will I design and administer assessments that help students understand how their test scores and grades are related to their status on the progression of knowledge they are expected to master?
Content	3. Conducting Direct Instruction Lessons	When content is new, how will I design and deliver direct instruction lessons that help students understand which parts are important and how the parts fit together?
	4. Conducting Practicing and Deepening Lessons	After presenting content, how will I design and deliver lessons that help students deepen their understanding and develop fluency in skills and processes?
	5. Conducting Knowledge Application Lessons	After presenting content, how will I design and deliver lessons that help students generate and defend claims through knowledge application?
	6. Using Strategies That Appear in All Types of Lessons	Throughout all types of lessons, what strategies will I use to help students continually integrate new knowledge with old knowledge and revise their understanding accordingly?

continued →

	Design Areas	Design Questions
Context	7. Using Engagement Strategies	What engagement strategies will I use to help students pay attention, be energized, be intrigued, and be inspired?
	8. Implementing Rules and Procedures	What strategies will I use to help students understand and follow rules and procedures?
	9. Building Relationships	What strategies will I use to help students feel welcome, accepted, and valued?
	10. Communicating High Expectations	What strategies will I use to help typically reluctant students feel valued and comfortable interacting with their peers and me?

Source: Marzano, 2017, pp. 6–7.

Within the ten categories of teacher actions, we have organized sets of strategies in even more fine-grained categories, called *elements*. As teachers think about each design question, they can then consider specific elements within the design area.

Forty-Three Elements

The forty-three elements provide detailed guidance about the nature and purpose of a category of strategies. Table I.3 depicts the elements that correspond to each design area. For example, the design area of *providing and communicating clear learning goals* involves three elements.

1. Providing scales and rubrics (element 1)
2. Tracking student progress (element 2)
3. Celebrating success (element 3)

As a teacher considers how to provide and communicate clear learning goals that help students understand the progression of knowledge he or she expects them to master and where they are along that progression (design question 1), the teacher might think more specifically about providing scales and rubrics, tracking student progress, and celebrating success. These are the elements within the first design area.

Finally, these forty-three elements encompass hundreds of specific instructional strategies, some of which we explore in this book in relation to the mathematics classroom. Table I.3 lists the forty-three separate elements in the *New Art and Science of Teaching* framework beneath their respective design areas.

The Need for Subject-Specific Models

General frameworks like *The New Art and Science of Teaching* certainly have their place in a teacher's understanding of effective instruction. However, a content-specific model of instruction can be a useful supplement to the more general framework in *The New Art and Science of Teaching*. The content-specific model should fit within the context of the general framework, but it should be based on content-specific research and should take into account the unique challenges of teaching a particular content area. For mathematics, such a content-specific model should address important aspects of mathematics and mathematics instruction, such as higher cognitive thinking, reasoning, and problem solving, and address the important concept areas of number sense, operations, measurement and data, and algebraic thinking. A content-specific model for mathematics should address these aspects in depth and relate back to the general framework of instruction. We designed this book to provide just such a model. Specifically, in the following chapters, we address the three overarching categories—(1) feedback, (2) content, and (3) context—with their corresponding ten categories of instruction and the embedded forty-three elements that feature specific strategies expressly for mathematics.

Table I.3: Elements Within the Ten Design Areas

Feedback	Content	Context
Providing and Communicating Clear Learning Goals 1. Providing scales and rubrics 2. Tracking student progress 3. Celebrating success **Using Assessments** 4. Using informal assessments of the whole class 5. Using formal assessments of individual students	**Conducting Direct Instruction Lessons** 6. Chunking content 7. Processing content 8. Recording and representing content **Conducting Practicing and Deepening Lessons** 9. Using structured practice sessions 10. Examining similarities and differences 11. Examining errors in reasoning **Conducting Knowledge Application Lessons** 12. Engaging students in cognitively complex tasks 13. Providing resources and guidance 14. Generating and defending claims **Using Strategies That Appear in All Types of Lessons** 15. Previewing strategies 16. Highlighting critical information 17. Reviewing content 18. Revising knowledge 19. Reflecting on learning 20. Assigning purposeful homework 21. Elaborating on information 22. Organizing students to interact	**Using Engagement Strategies** 23. Noticing and reacting when students are not engaged 24. Increasing response rates 25. Using physical movement 26. Maintaining a lively pace 27. Demonstrating intensity and enthusiasm 28. Presenting unusual information 29. Using friendly controversy 30. Using academic games 31. Providing opportunities for students to talk about themselves 32. Motivating and inspiring students **Implementing Rules and Procedures** 33. Establishing rules and procedures 34. Organizing the physical layout of the classroom 35. Demonstrating withitness 36. Acknowledging adherence to rules and procedures 37. Acknowledging lack of adherence to rules and procedures **Building Relationships** 38. Using verbal and nonverbal behaviors that indicate affection for students 39. Understanding students' backgrounds and interests 40. Displaying objectivity and control **Communicating High Expectations** 41. Demonstrating value and respect for reluctant learners 42. Asking in-depth questions of reluctant learners 43. Probing incorrect answers with reluctant learners

Source: Marzano, 2017, p. 8.

Although this text predominantly provides suggestions to support lesson planning around mathematics instruction, we encourage readers to explore the foundational book *The New Art and Science of Teaching* (Marzano, 2017). In doing so, they will likely infuse their content areas and grade levels with additional strategies.

About This Book

In chapters 1 through 10, we situate a mathematics-specific model within the broader context of *The New Art and Science of Teaching* framework. Part I, focused on feedback, begins with chapter 1, which describes how teachers can effectively articulate learning goals for mathematics content within scales and rubrics, create learning progressions (called proficiency scales), and use those scales to track students' progress and celebrate their success. In chapter 2, we explain strategies for how to assess students' current mathematics status using both informal and formal assessment.

Part II addresses content. In chapters 3, 4, 5, and 6, we articulate instructional strategies for teaching the mathematics content that students need to learn. Chapter 3 focuses on conducting direct instruction lessons, chapter 4 on conducting practicing and deepening lessons, chapter 5 on conducting knowledge application lessons, and chapter 6 on using strategies that appear in all types of lessons.

Part III, concentrated on context, reviews mathematics-related issues pertaining to student engagement (chapter 7), rules and procedures (chapter 8), building relationships (chapter 9), and communicating high expectations to all students (chapter 10).

Chapter 11 describes a four-step process for developing teachers' expertise. In anticipation of chapter 11, each chapter contains self-rating scales for readers to assess their performance on the elements of the model. By doing this, they can determine their areas of strength and the areas in which they might want to improve relative to *The New Art and Science of Teaching*. All of the self-rating scales in this book have the same format for progression of development. To introduce these scales and help readers understand them, we present the general format of a self-rating scale in figure I.2.

Score	Description
4: Innovating	I adapt strategies and behaviors associated with this element for unique student needs and situations.
3: Applying	I use strategies and behaviors associated with this element without significant errors and monitor their effect on students.
2: Developing	I use strategies and behaviors associated with this element without significant errors but do not monitor their effect on students.
1: Beginning	I use some strategies and behaviors associated with this element but do so with significant errors or omissions.
0: Not Using	I am unaware of the strategies and behaviors associated with this element or know them but don't employ them.

Figure I.2: General format of the self-rating scale.

To understand this scale, it is best to start at the bottom with the Not Using row. Here, the teacher is unaware of the strategies that relate to the element or knows them but doesn't employ them. At the Beginning level, the teacher uses strategies that relate to the element, but leaves out important parts or makes significant mistakes. At the Developing level, the teacher executes strategies important to the element without significant errors or omissions but does not monitor their effect on students. At the Applying level, the teacher not only executes strategies without significant errors or omissions but also monitors students to ensure that they are experiencing the desired effects. We consider the Applying level the level at which one can legitimately expect tangible results in students. Finally, at the Innovating level, the teacher is aware of and makes any adaptations to the strategies for students who require such an arrangement.

Each chapter also contains Guiding Questions for Curriculum Design to support planning and aid in reflection. Appendix A provides an overview of *The New Art and Science of Teaching* framework. Appendix

B, Lesson Seed: Fluency With the Solute Game, provides details for a game to support student fluency in mathematics. Appendix C provides a list of tables and figures.

In sum, *The New Art and Science of Teaching Mathematics* is designed to present a mathematics-specific model of instruction within the context of *The New Art and Science of Teaching* framework. We address thirty-five elements from the general model within the context of mathematics instruction and provide mathematics-specific strategies and techniques that teachers can use to improve their effectiveness and elicit desired mental states and processes from their students.

PART I
Feedback

CHAPTER 1

Providing and Communicating Clear Learning Goals

The New Art and Science of Teaching framework begins by addressing how teachers will communicate with students about what they need to learn. It addresses the teacher question, *How will I communicate clear learning goals that help students understand the progression of knowledge in mathematics they are expected to master and where they are along that progression?*

This design area includes three elements related to tracking students' progress and celebrating their success. Together, these three elements—(1) providing scales and rubrics, (2) tracking student progress, and (3) celebrating success—create a foundation for effective feedback. In this chapter, we describe specific strategies for implementing these elements in a mathematics classroom.

Scales and rubrics are essential for tracking student progress, and tracking progress is necessary for celebrating success. The desired joint effect of the strategies associated with these three elements is that students understand the progression of knowledge they are expected to master and where they currently are along that progression. When learning goals are designed well and communicated well, students not only have clear direction, but they can take the reins of their own learning. As Robert J. Marzano (2017) articulates in *The New Art and Science of Teaching*, students must grasp the scaffolding of knowledge and skills they are expected to master and understand where they are in the learning, and this happens as a result of the teacher providing and communicating clear learning goals.

Element 1: Providing Scales and Rubrics

Scales and rubrics articulate what students should know and be able to do as a result of instruction. The content in a scale or rubric should come from a school or district's standards. As an example of how teachers might do this, we include the learning progression for mathematics from Achieve the Core (n.d.) in figure 1.1 (page 12) and in figure 1.2 (page 13) for secondary-level mathematics.

For element 1 of the model, we address the following two specific strategies in this chapter.

1. Clearly articulating learning goals
2. Creating scales or rubrics for learning goals

K	Understand addition as putting together and adding to, and understand subtraction as taking apart and taking from. Work with numbers 11–19 to gain foundations for place value.	Know number names and the count sequence. Count to tell the number of objects. Compare numbers.
Grade 1	Extend the counting sequence. Understand place value. Use place value understanding and properties of operations to add and subtract. Measure lengths indirectly and by iterating length units.	Represent and solve problems involving addition and subtraction. Understand and apply properties of operations and the relationship between addition and subtraction. Add and subtract within 20. Work with addition and subtraction equations.
Grade 2	Use place value understanding and properties of operations to add and subtract. Measure and estimate lengths in standard units. Relate addition and subtraction to length.	Represent and solve problems involving addition and subtraction. Add and subtract within 20. Understand place value.
Grade 3	Develop understanding of fractions as numbers. Solve problems involving measurement and estimation of intervals of time, liquid volumes, and masses of objects. Geometric measurement: understand concepts of area, and relate area to multiplication and to addition.	Represent and solve problems involving multiplication and division. Understand properties of multiplication and the relationship between multiplication and division. Multiply and divide within 100. Solve problems involving the four operations, and identify and explain patterns in arithmetic.
Grade 4	Extend understanding of fraction equivalence and ordering. Build fractions from unit fractions by applying and extending previous understandings of operations. Understand decimal notation for fractions, and compare decimal fractions.	Use the four operations with whole numbers to solve problems. Generalize place value understanding for multidigit whole numbers. Use place value understanding and properties of operations to perform multidigit arithmetic.
Grade 5	Geometric measurement: understand concepts of volume and relate volume to multiplication and to addition. Graph points in the coordinate plane to solve real-world and mathematical problems.	Understand the place value system. Perform operations with multidigit whole numbers and decimals to hundredths. Use equivalent fractions as a strategy to add and subtract fractions. Apply and extend previous understandings of multiplication and division to multiply and divide fractions.
Grade 6	Apply and extend previous understandings of arithmetic to algebraic expressions. Reason about and solve one-variable equations and inequalities. Represent and analyze quantitative relationships between dependent and independent variables.	Apply and extend previous understandings of multiplication and division to divide fractions by fractions. Apply and extend previous understandings of numbers to the system of rational numbers. Understand ratio concepts, and use ratio reasoning to solve problems.

Grade 7	Apply and extend previous understanding of operations with fractions to add, subtract, multiply, and divide rational numbers. Analyze proportional relationships and use them to solve real-world and mathematical problems. Use properties of operations to generate equivalent expressions. Solve real-life and mathematical problems using numerical and algebraic expressions and equations.
Grade 8	Work with radical and integer exponents. Understand the connections between proportional relationships, lines, and linear equations. Analyze and solve linear equations and pairs of simultaneous linear equations. Define, evaluate, and compare functions. Use functions to model relationships between quantities.

Source: Achieve the Core, (n.d.).

Figure 1.1: Learning progression for mathematics, grades K-8.

Number and Quantity	Algebra	Functions	Geometry	Statistics and Probability	Applying Key Takeaways from Grades 6-8
N-RN, Real Numbers: Both clusters in this domain contain widely applicable prerequisites. **N-Q*, Quantities:** Every standard in this domain is a widely applicable prerequisite. Note, this domain is especially important in the high school content standards overall as a widely applicable prerequisite.	**Every domain in this category** contains widely applicable prerequisites. Note, the **A-SSE** domain is especially important in the high school content standards overall as a widely applicable prerequisite.	**F-IF, Interpreting Functions:** Every cluster in this domain contains widely applicable prerequisites. Additionally, standards **F-BF.1** and **F-LE.1** are relatively important within this category as widely applicable prerequisites.	**The following standards and clusters** are relatively important within this category as widely applicable prerequisites: G-CO.1, G-CO.9, G-CO.10, G-SRT.B, G-SRT.C Note, the above standards in turn have learning prerequisites within the Geometry category, including: G-CO.A, G-CO.B, G-SRT.A	**The following standards** are relatively important within this category as widely applicable prerequisites: S-ID.2, S-ID.7, S-IC.1 Note, the above standards in turn have learning prerequisites within 6-8.SP.	**Solving problems at a level of sophistication appropriate to high school by:** • Applying ratios and proportional relationships. • Applying percentages and unit conversions, e.g., in the context of complicated measurement problems involving quantities with derived or compound units (such as mg/mL, kg/m³, acre-feet, etc.). • Applying basic function concepts, e.g., by interpreting the features of a graph in the context of an applied problem. • Applying concepts and skills of geometric measurement e.g., when analyzing a diagram or schematic. • Applying concepts and skills of basic statistics and probability (see 6-8.SP). • Performing rational number arithmetic fluently.

Source: National Governors Association Center for Best Practices & Council of Chief State School Officers, 2013.

Figure 1.2: Learning progression for mathematics, secondary level.

Clearly Articulating Learning Goals

Mathematics learning goals are most effective when teachers communicate them in a way students can clearly understand; however, students must also feel as though they "own" the goals. Student ownership is the process of allowing students the freedom to choose their goals and take responsibility for measuring their progress toward meeting them. Student ownership occurs most effectively when students are able to connect to mathematics using natural, everyday language. Stephen Chappuis and Richard J. Stiggins (2002) explain that sharing learning goals in student-friendly language at the outset of a lesson is the critical first step in helping students know where they are going. They also point out that students cannot assess their own learning (see element 2, tracking student progress, page 18) or set goals to work toward without a clear vision of the intended learning. When they do try to assess their own achievement without understanding the learning targets they have been working toward, their conclusions can't help them move forward.

The following three actions will help teachers communicate learning goals effectively so that students can connect to mathematics.

1. **Eliminating jargon:** Eliminate jargon that is intended for the teacher and instead incorporate empowering language that provides focus and motivation.
2. **Making goals concrete:** Communicate learning goals with vivid and concrete language.
3. **Using imagery and multiple representations:** Promote mathematics concepts as visually connected to numerical values and symbols.

Table 1.1 provides some examples of these three actions.

Table 1.1: Actions for Communicating Learning Goals

Strategy	Description
Eliminating jargon	Instead of using the language from the standard to create the learning target, use vocabulary and terminology that make sense and are motivating, and then explicitly teach new vocabulary words.
Making goals concrete	Use language that clarifies what the student is doing and how.
Using imagery and multiple representations	Encourage students to represent their mathematics learning goals in different forms, such as with words, a picture, a graph, an equation, or a concrete object, and encourage students to link the different forms.

Eliminating Jargon

Learning goals can be difficult for students to grasp when they contain pedagogical jargon and seem to be crafted more for education experts than for students. We don't mean to discredit the use of academic language; however, when academic language becomes a barrier because it prevents students from connecting with the material, teachers have to re-evaluate how they're communicating about mathematics. When learning goals are ambiguous, they don't provide the focus, motivation, or inspiration students need to reach targets. Mathematics teachers must align learning goal language to desired learning outcomes for students using everyday language and connect it to academic language by showing the students the goal written in various ways. Judit Moschkovich (2012) states that instruction needs to move away from a monolithic view of mathematical discourse and consider everyday and academic discourses as interdependent, dialectical, and related rather than assume they are mutually exclusive. Additionally, learning goals should make appropriate connections to academic language when scaffolding is present. Figure 1.3 shows a standard followed by the rewritten student-friendly, jargon-free statement for two grade levels and algebra II.

Grade 5 **Standard:** Students will classify two-dimensional shapes. **Student-friendly version:** I can identify and sort quadrilaterals.
Grade 8 **Standard:** Analyze and solve pairs of simultaneous linear equations. **Student-friendly version**: I can make connections between the problem-solving strategies used in a baseball task and some algebraic strategies that I can use to solve problems involving systems of equations.
Algebra 2 **Standard:** Graph polynomial functions, identifying zeros when suitable factorizations are available, and showing end behavior. **Student-friendly version:** I can represent a polynomial function on a graph. A polynomial is an expression that can have constants (like 4), variables (like x or y) and exponents (like the 2 in y^2), that can be combined using addition, subtraction, multiplication, and division.

Figure 1.3: Transforming a learning goal by eliminating jargon.

Obtaining student feedback is the best way to determine if learning goals make sense to students. Creating a focus group of students (a committee to eliminate jargon) that vet learning goals is a strategy to ensure your learning goals are student friendly. In this process, the teacher asks students in the focus group to circle nouns and verbs that seem ambiguous or don't seem very connected to everyday language.

Figure 1.4 is an example of how a student focus group would provide feedback on the first draft of a learning goal.

Teacher-proposed learning goal: I can use the commutative property to find the product of a multiplication problem.
Focus group feedback: "I don't remember what the commutative property is." "Is this the same as the break-apart strategy?" "Is this where I break numbers so I can better see how to multiply them?" "What kind of multiplication problem?"
New goal based on student feedback: I can use the break-apart strategy to multiply two numbers.

Figure 1.4: Transforming a learning goal with student feedback.

The students from the group in figure 1.4 had previously learned the break-apart strategy and were able to relate to it. Because the break-apart strategy is indeed a commutative strategy, the teacher incorporated student feedback and instead used the terminology students were familiar with in the updated learning goal. It was not as important for students to know the word *commutative* as it was for them to be able to connect a problem (multiplying two numbers) to how they would solve it (the break-apart strategy). A great time for seeking feedback for eliminating jargon is before collaborative planning sessions. Teachers can provide a list of upcoming learning goals to students and develop an interactive game where students suggest alternate nouns or verbs. The teachers then bring the feedback to collaborative planning time for discussion and implementation.

Making Goals Concrete

According to researchers Sean M. McCrea, Nira Liberman, Yaacov Trope, and Steven J. Sherman (2008), people who think about the future in concrete rather than abstract terms are less likely to procrastinate. This is because a vivid picture of the future makes it seem more real and thus easier to prioritize. Learning goals are pictures of the future; they must appear in concrete language so students feel motivated to meet them. Figure 1.5 shows a learning goal stated in student-friendly language revised to be more concrete.

Grade 3 **Student-friendly language:** I can determine the unknown whole number in a multiplication or division equation. **Using concrete language:** I can determine the unknown in a multiplication problem and justify the strategy I used while playing the *Salute* card game.
Grades 4–8 **Student-friendly language:** I can construct viable arguments and critique the reasoning of others. **Using concrete language:** I can share my thinking about shapes and their properties without the fear of being wrong, because every answer is correct as long as you can justify your reasoning through the Which One Doesn't Belong? graphic organizer.
Algebra 2 **Student-friendly language:** I can graph polynomial functions. **Using concrete language:** Using a graphic calculator in my gallery walk group, I can identify similarities and differences in the four polynomial graphs I created.

Figure 1.5: Transforming a learning goal by using concrete language.

In the examples in figure 1.5, the original learning goals don't specify what kind of problem the student is solving, and they don't identify a particular strategy to determine the unknown. The intention of "I can" learning targets is to increase clarity by homing in on intended learning.

Additionally, in mathematics instruction, teachers should explicitly communicate technology tools within the learning goals that can enhance the learning. Will students have the option of using a collaborative digital tool to reason through a problem or will they be solving the problem on a sheet of paper? An example of a learning goal with the use of technology is, "I can solve word problems using fractions and show my thinking by creating a video representation."

Using Imagery and Multiple Representations

Using imagery and representations in mathematics means presenting information in the form of a diagram or chart, for example, or representing information as a mental picture with a concrete image. Visual representation strategies are important for students as they help to support student learning in mathematics for different types of problems. Researchers note that the ways we posture, gaze, gesture, point, and use tools when expressing mathematical ideas are evidence that we hold mathematical ideas in the motor and perceptual areas of the brain—which is now supported by brain evidence (Nemirovsky, Rasmussen, Sweeney, & Wawro, 2012). The researchers point out that when we explain ideas, even when we don't have the words we need, we tend to draw shapes in the air (Nemirovsky et al., 2012). According to Boaler (2016), we use visual pathways when we work on mathematics, and we all need to develop the visual areas of our brains. One problem with mathematics in schools is that teachers present it as a subject of numbers and symbols, ignoring the potential of visual mathematics for transforming students' mathematical experiences and developing important neural pathways. The National Council of Teachers of Mathematics (NCTM) has long advocated the use of multiple representations in students' learning of mathematics (see Kirwan & Tobias, 2014; Tripathi, 2014). But in many classrooms, teachers still employ the traditional approach of mathematics instruction focused on numbers and symbols. To ensure students develop understanding of mathematics through multiple representations, teachers must ensure that learning goals address this strategy.

The example in figure 1.6, derived from Boaler's (2016) research, shows how to transform a learning goal using visualization through imagery.

Student-friendly language: I can use multiplication within 100 to solve word problems in situations involving equal groups, arrays, and measurement quantities.
Using imagery: Starting with a blank 100-box grid, I will play a dice game that will provide the numbers I will use to fill in my array. From the array, I will create a corresponding number sentence. An example of my array would look like:
Student-friendly language: I can classify two-dimensional shapes.
Using imagery: Using a card sort, I will organize an assortment of shapes—quadrilaterals, nonquadrilaterals, regular polygons, and not regular polygons—into the four different categories on a grid.
Student-friendly language: I can graph polynomial functions.
Using imagery: I can compare four different polynomial function equations, tables, and graphs with others in class. I can identify the similarities and differences with the graphs or equations. I also notice similarities between polynomial functions and functions that we have discussed before in class.

Figure 1.6: Transforming a learning goal using imagery.

In the first example in figure 1.6, using imagery to transform a learning goal allows students to visualize how they will represent a multiplication problem with an array. Many learning goals call for the use of arrays or a visual representation, but this isn't always meaningful for students unless they see an example right from the beginning of, and throughout, the lesson until they have built understanding.

When teachers communicate learning goals, it's important that the communication extends beyond a written statement visible in the classroom or on a device. Carla Jensen, Tamara Whitehouse, and Rachael Coulehan (2000) find that teachers can support students in connecting to mathematical terminology and symbolic notation through verbal communication. The dialogic nature of communicating about mathematics supports students in accessing new mathematical terms and processes.

Creating Scales or Rubrics for Learning Goals

An effective tool for creating rubrics and accessing standards-based rubrics is the free online tool ThemeSpark Rubric Maker (www.themespark.net). To measure mathematical thinking, you might want to create a scale for a specific skill like reasoning, problem-solving, or perseverance. Figure 1.7, adapted from Engage NY (2013), shows a rating scale for the skill of reasoning.

Falls Far Below Learning Standard	Approaches Learning Standard	Meets Learning Standard	Exceeds Learning Standard
1	2	3	4
The answer is missing or incorrect, and there is little evidence of reasoning or application of mathematics to solve the problem.	The answer is missing or incorrect, but there is evidence of some reasoning or application of mathematics to solve the problem.	The answer is correct with some evidence of reasoning or application of mathematics to solve the problem, or the answer is incorrect, but there is substantial evidence of solid reasoning or application of mathematics to solve the problem.	The answer is correct, and substantial evidence of solid reasoning or application of mathematics to solve the problem supports it.

Source: Adapted from Engage NY, 2013.

Figure 1.7: Rating scale for reasoning.

We recommend that teachers use the scale in figure 1.8 (page 18) to rate their current level of effectiveness with providing scales and rubrics.

Score	Description
4: Innovating	I adapt behaviors and create new strategies for unique student needs and situations.
3: Applying	I provide scales and rubrics, and I monitor the extent to which my actions affect students' performance.
2: Developing	I provide scales and rubrics, but I do not monitor the effect on students.
1: Beginning	I use the strategies and behaviors associated with this element incorrectly or with parts missing.
0: Not Using	I am unaware of strategies and behaviors associated with this element.

Figure 1.8: Self-rating scale for element 1—Providing scales and rubrics.

Element 2: Tracking Student Progress

Tracking student progress in the mathematics classroom is similar to tracking student progress in any content area: the student receives a score based on a proficiency scale, and the teacher uses the student's pattern of scores to "provide each student with a clear sense of where he or she started relative to a topic and where he or she is currently" (Marzano, 2017, p. 14). For each topic at each applicable grade level, teachers should construct a proficiency scale (or learning progression). Such a scale allows teachers to pinpoint where a student falls on a continuum of knowledge, using information from assessments. A generic proficiency scale format appears in figure 1.9.

4.0	**More complex content**
3.5	In addition to score 3.0 performance, partial success at score 4.0 content
3.0	**Target content**
2.5	No major errors or omissions regarding score 2.0 content, and partial success at score 3.0 content
2.0	**Simpler content**
1.5	Partial success at score 2.0 content, and major errors or omissions regarding score 3.0 content
1.0	**With help, partial success at score 2.0 content and score 3.0 content**
0.5	With help, partial success at score 2.0 content but not at score 3.0 content
0.0	**Even with help, no success**

Figure 1.9: Generic format for a proficiency scale.

The proficiency scale format in figure 1.9 is designed so that the only descriptors that change from one scale to the next are those at the 2.0, 3.0, and 4.0 levels. Those levels articulate target content, simpler content, and more complex content. Teachers draw target content from standards documents; simpler content and more complex content elaborate on the target content. For example, figure 1.10 shows a proficiency scale for a grade 8 mathematics standard.

4.0	The student will: Solve problems by applying the understanding that a function is a rule that assigns to each input exactly one output. The graph of a function is the set of ordered pairs consisting of an input and the corresponding output.
3.5	In addition to score 3.0 performance, students have partial success at score 4.0 content.
3.0	The student will: Explain that a function is a rule that assigns to each input exactly one output. The graph of a function is the set of ordered pairs consisting of an input and the corresponding output.

2.5	The student has no major errors or omissions regarding score 2.0 content and partial success at score 3.0 content.
2.0	The student remembers that a function is a rule that assigns to each input exactly one output.
1.5	The student has partial success at score 2.0 content and major errors or omissions regarding score 3.0 content.
1.0	With help, the student has partial success at score 2.0 content and score 3.0 content.
0.5	With help, the student has partial success at score 2.0 content but not at score 3.0 content.
0.0	Even with help, the student has no success.

Figure 1.10: Proficiency scale for graphing functions at grade 8.

The elements at the 3.0 level describe what the student does essentially as the learning standard states. The 2.0 level articulates simpler content for each of these elements, and the 4.0 level articulates beyond what the teacher taught.

Figure 1.11 shows an individual student's progress on one topic for which there is a proficiency scale. The student began with a score of 1.5 but increased his or her score to 3.5 over five assessments. The strategy of using formative scores throughout a unit of instruction helps teachers and students monitor progress and adjust if necessary. This is different from summative scores, which represent a student's status at the end of a particular point in time. To collect formative scores over time that pertain to a specific proficiency scale, the mathematics teacher uses the strategy of utilizing different types of assessments, including obtrusive assessments (which interrupt the flow of classroom activity), unobtrusive assessments (which do not interrupt classroom activities), or student-generated assessments.

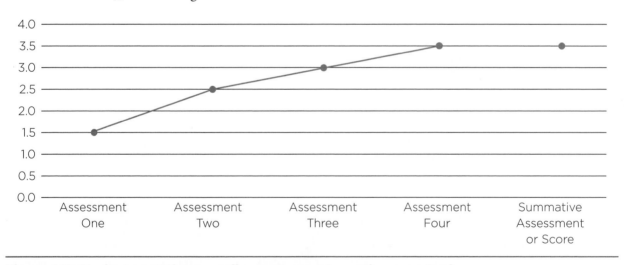

Figure 1.11: Student growth across five assessments on the same topic.

For further guidance regarding the construction and use of proficiency scales, see *Formative Assessment and Standards-Based Grading* (Marzano, 2010a) and *Making Classroom Assessment Reliable and Valid* (Marzano, 2018). By clearly articulating different levels of performance relative to the target content, both teachers and the students themselves can describe and track students' progress. They can use a line graph or bar graph of the data to show students' growth over time.

Figure 1.12 (page 20) shows a student proficiency scale with a self-reflection component for planning. This can help with the strategy of charting student progress as a student sets a goal relative to a specific scale at the beginning of a unit or grading period and then tracks his or her scores on that scale. At the end of the unit or grading period, the teacher assigns a final, or summative, score to the student for the scale.

I can find the area of a rectangle.			
	This means I can:	**What I Can Do**	**My Plan to Learn**
4	Find a missing side length on a rectangle if I know its area, and finds two or more different rectangles that have the same area.		
3	Find the area of the rectangle using a formula and explain why the formula works.		
2	Find the area of a rectangle by making an array and counting the unit squares.		
1	Find the area of a rectangle by counting unit squares.		

Figure 1.12: Student proficiency scale for self-rating and planning.

*Visit **go.SolutionTree.com/instruction** for a free reproducible version of this figure.*

We recommend that teachers use the scale in figure 1.13 to rate their current level of effectiveness with element 2, tracking student progress.

Score	Description
4: Innovating	I adapt behaviors and create new strategies for unique student needs and situations.
3: Applying	I track student progress, and I monitor the extent to which my actions affect student learning.
2: Developing	I track student progress, but I do not monitor the effect on student learning.
1: Beginning	I use the strategies and behaviors associated with this element incorrectly or with parts missing.
0: Not Using	I am unaware of strategies and behaviors associated with this element.

Figure 1.13: Self-rating scale for element 2—Tracking student progress.

Element 3: Celebrating Success

Celebrating success in the mathematics classroom should focus on students' progress on proficiency scales. That is, teachers should celebrate students for their growth. This may differ from what teachers traditionally celebrate in the classroom. For instance, a teacher might be used to celebrating how many mathematics problems students can answer correctly in three minutes, the winner of math drills, or how well students perform on a standardized test. While there may be benefits to these types of celebrations, they are not as conducive to reliable measurement as progress on a proficiency scale, which allows the teacher to celebrate knowledge gain—the difference between a student's initial and final scores for a learning goal. To celebrate knowledge gain, the teacher recognizes the growth each student has made over the course of a unit. Mathematics teachers can also use the strategies of status celebration (celebrating students' status at any point in time) and verbal feedback (emphasizing achievement and growth by verbally explaining what a student has done well) throughout the unit.

Figure 1.14 presents the self-rating scale for element 3, celebrating success.

Score	Description
4: Innovating	I adapt behaviors and create new strategies for unique student needs and situations.
3: Applying	I celebrate success, and I monitor the extent to which my actions affect students.
2: Developing	I celebrate success, but I do not monitor the effect on students.
1: Beginning	I use the strategies and behaviors associated with this element incorrectly or with parts missing.
0: Not Using	I am unaware of strategies and behaviors associated with this element.

Figure 1.14: Self-rating scale for element 3—Celebrating success.

GUIDING QUESTIONS FOR CURRICULUM DESIGN

When teachers engage in curriculum design, they consider this overarching question for communicating clear goals and objectives: *How will I communicate clear learning goals that help students understand the progression of knowledge they are expected to master and where they are along that progression?* Consider the following questions aligned to the elements in this chapter to guide your planning.

- **Element 1:** How will I design scales and rubrics?

  _____

  _____

  _____

  _____

  _____

  _____

- **Element 2:** How will I track student progress?

  _____

  _____

  _____

  _____

  _____

  _____

- **Element 3:** How will I celebrate success?

  _____

  _____

  _____

  _____

  _____

  _____

Summary

Providing and communicating clear learning goals involves three elements: (1) providing scales and rubrics, (2) tracking student progress, and (3) celebrating success. In the mathematics classroom, how teachers state these learning goals can make the difference between students reaching proficiency or not. They can support students in thinking in complex ways about mathematics, but only if they are communicated in a way that students understand and that inspires them to solve problems. Tracking student progress and celebrating success is not only important in the classroom but crucial in mathematics, as students are continually pursuing perseverance in problem solving and need support and affirmation to help them along the way.

CHAPTER 2

Using Assessments

The second design area from *The New Art and Science of Teaching* framework involves the use of effective assessments. Some mathematics teachers use assessments only as evaluation tools to quantify students' current status relative to specific knowledge and skills. While this is certainly a legitimate use of assessments, the primary purpose should be to provide students with feedback they can use to improve. When mathematics teachers use assessments to their full capacity, students understand how their test scores and grades relate to their status on specific progressions of knowledge and skills teachers expect them to master.

Element 4, using informal assessments of the whole class, and element 5, using formal assessments of individual students, together allow teachers to monitor student progress, provide useful feedback, and ensure that all students are moving toward mastery of the content. Here, we describe how these elements might manifest in a mathematics classroom.

Element 4: Using Informal Assessments of the Whole Class

In the mathematics classroom, teachers create and use informal formative assessments to monitor student progress in order to differentiate instruction, reteach concepts and skills, address misconceptions, and to provide meaningful feedback. In this section, we describe the use of three specific strategies for informal assessment of the whole class in the mathematics classroom.

1. Virtual exit slips
2. Guided reciprocal peer questioning
3. Respond, summarize, question, connect, and comment (RSQC2)

Teachers can use these tools as response strategies for students when students are to address a question or prompt and for the strategy of unrecorded assessment, in which teachers use the assessment for feedback but not to score students.

Virtual Exit Slips

Exit slips are student responses to questions teachers pose at the conclusion of an instructional activity in which students reflect on the learning. Exit slips are an effective way to quickly assess students' level of understanding and set up for the next learning opportunity. Marzano (2012) articulates at least four ways teachers can use exit slips, each having a different intended outcome.

1. To rate students' current understanding of new learning
2. To analyze and reflect on students' efforts around the learning
3. To provide feedback to teachers on a respective strategy
4. To provide feedback about the instruction and instructional resources

Virtual exit slips—those that use technology—can transform the way formative assessments take place in the mathematics classroom. Virtual exit slips provide the teacher with a more effective way of assessing student learning, because the feedback is immediate, interactive, and can be more efficiently tracked and saved. As with traditional exit slips, with virtual exit slips, teachers pose a question or prompt at the conclusion of a learning block or lesson, and students have the opportunity to respond. The difference is that rather than using paper and pencil, students respond through a variety of virtual tools, such as WeVideo, Flipgrid, Adobe Spark, and Canva, to name a few.

- **WeVideo (www.wevideo.com):** A creativity platform that allows students to create videos to deepen learning experiences
- **Flipgrid (https://flipgrid.com):** An online tool for sharing and discussion that facilitates students recording videos and replying to one another
- **Adobe Spark (https://spark.adobe.com):** An online platform that allows students to create beautiful presentations
- **Canva (www.canva.com):** An online tool that makes it possible to design anything and publish anywhere with thousands of customizable templates.

With these tools, students are able to reflect on mathematical thinking, create visual representations of mathematics concepts, or create mathematics videos. Students then post their responses through a district-approved and Children's Online Privacy Protection Act (COPPA)-compliant platform with teacher guidance, such as on the class learning management system (LMS), or share their responses via district-approved social media outlets (such as Twitter, Facebook, Instagram, and so on). Virtual exit slips using tools such as those listed tap into student creativity. Students are intrinsically motivated to respond because they have choices (responding digitally in a medium they prefer) in the visual and text creation and they feel pride in sharing their creations online.

Virtual exit slips also allow mathematics teachers to provide input and feedback quickly to individual students (because cloud-based feedback tools allow for real-time, synchronous feedback), and teachers can then appropriately adjust instruction, properly scaffolding and sequencing the next day's content in meaningful ways.

For the exit slip to be formative, there must be teacher and student action on the information. For example, the teacher must review answers, sort the results into groups (got it, almost got it, not yet), and then give each group a specific problem to begin the lesson the next day.

Figure 2.1 provides some prompts and sample responses from virtual exit slips in the mathematics classroom that teachers can administer virtually using Google Docs or other technology.

Guided Reciprocal Peer Questioning

Formative assessments should not only provide teachers with quick and ongoing checks for understanding but should also provide students with opportunities to learn while being assessed. During guided reciprocal peer questioning, students build inquiry skills while they go through the process of constructing questions. At the same time, they also develop metacognition skills through reflection. Teachers can provide scaffolding for this strategy by first issuing question prompts for students to choose from and then eventually asking students to create their own prompts. To aid in question generation, it's useful to refer to the learning protocol of building probing questions. Former economist and educator Charlotte Danielson (2011) developed a

Grade 3: Suppose students know that the bus arrives at their home at 6:45 a.m. Students need to develop reasoning (and their parents would be grateful!) about how much time is needed for the student to awake and be ready for the bus pickup. Is fifteen minutes enough time? Is forty-five minutes enough time?

Grade 7: YoYo Yogurt sells yogurt at a price based upon the total weight of the yogurt and the toppings in a dish. Each member of Gia's famly weighed his or her dish and paid the corresponding amount shown in the chart below.

Cost ($)	5	4	2	3.20
Weight (oz)	12.5	10	5	8

Does everyone pay the same cost per ounce? Show your work and explain how you know.

Is the cost proportional to the weight? Explain your answer.

High school: The equation of a circle in the xy-plane is shown below. What is the diameter of the circle? Be sure to show your work and explain your answer.

$x^2 + y^2 - 6x + 8y = 144$

Source: Kanold, Larson, Fennell, Adams, Dixon, Kobett, & Wray, 2012.

Figure 2.1: Prompts and sample responses using virtual exit slips.

framework for teaching that includes five mediational questions that teachers can use for guided reciprocal peer questioning.

1. Why do you think this is the case?
2. What would you have to change in order for . . . ?
3. What do you assume to be true about . . . ?
4. How did you conclude . . . ?
5. How did your assumptions about _____ influence how you thought about . . . ?

For guided reciprocal peer questioning, teachers provide prompts during small-group collaborative learning and the appropriate amount of time (ten to fifteen minutes) to conduct the assessment. As students are discussing the prompts, the teacher circulates and records observations. Another key component of this strategy is capturing student reflection and thinking. Students can answer using voice recording, collaborative digital documents, notecards, and so on.

Respond, Summarize, Question, Connect, and Comment

RSQC2 is another formative assessment strategy that builds student thinking and learning while also providing teachers with evidence to check for learning. This protocol is unique in that it is structured to emulate the levels of Bloom's taxonomy (remember, understand, apply, analyze, evaluate, and create; Bloom, 1956). Additionally, the strategy to assess student knowledge is more effective because it not only focuses on connecting new concepts but also on building on previously learned concepts. It drives learning and captures progress. Following are the five steps for RSQC2.

1. **Recall:** Students make a list of what they recall as most important from a previous learning.
2. **Summarize:** Students summarize the essence of previous learning.
3. **Question:** Students ask one or two questions that still remain unanswered or that they are unclear about.

4. **Connect:** Students briefly explain the essential points and how they relate to their overall mathematics learning goals.

5. **Comment:** Students evaluate and share feedback about the previous learning.

Figure 2.2 shows a sample of potential responses from a student engaging with this protocol.

Student Name: Luis G.
Recall: From grade 4, I learned about right triangles, and I know how to classify two-dimensional shapes from the presence or absence of parallel or perpendicular lines.
Summarize: I can classify two-dimensional figures based on properties. I can now sort a variety of polygons by the number of parallel sides.
Question: How do I consistently tell the difference between a rhombus and a parallelogram?
Connect: Since the warm-up started with asking me to sort polygons based on parallel sides, the next task will ask me to take it one step further. I will identify another way I could potentially sort the same shapes.
Comment: When I struggled with sorting shapes, my teacher thought it was helpful to ask me what else I noticed about the shapes besides just the parallel sides, and what I noticed about the angles or side lengths.

Figure 2.2: RSQC2 informal assessment responses.

This strategy is well suited for virtual use in the mathematics classroom. Virtual collaboration allows for synchronous recording of thoughts and feedback from the teacher. Students can use a collaborative, shared document, such as OneNote Online or Google Docs, that the teacher and students have access to. Teachers can also encourage students to use social media tools, such as Twitter, Instagram, Edmodo, Google Classroom, and so on, to express their thinking. This is a motivational strategy, as most students enjoy expressing their thoughts on social media. Although formative-assessment data should be kept private, teachers should encourage students to reflect on their thinking and refine it. Sharing thoughts publically can encourage others to rethink how to approach and solve problems.

Figure 2.3 presents the self-rating scale for element 4, using informal assessments of the whole class, so teachers can gauge their professional performance.

Score	Description
4: Innovating	I adapt behaviors and create new strategies for unique student needs and situations.
3: Applying	I use informal assessments of the whole class to determine students' proficiency with specific content, and I monitor the extent to which students respond to assessment-guided feedback and instruction.
2: Developing	I use informal assessments of the whole class to determine students' proficiency with specific content, but I do not monitor the effect on students.
1: Beginning	I use the strategies and behaviors associated with this element incorrectly or with parts missing.
0: Not Using	I am unaware of strategies and behaviors associated with this element.

Figure 2.3: Self-rating scale for element 4—Using informal assessments of the whole class.

Element 5: Using Formal Assessments of Individual Students

Mathematics teachers create and utilize formal assessments to reliably record student learning data, provide feedback on student work, and create dynamic portfolios of student progress and growth. Formal assessments via performance tasks and portfolios inform teaching and learning while using strategies that take a comprehensive snapshot of where a student is in his or her learning.

For this element, we examine two formal assessment tools for teachers to use in the mathematics classroom for individual student assessment. These tools fit within the *The New Art and Science of Teaching* framework strategies for element 5 for student demonstrations (students generate presentations that demonstrate their understanding of a topic, usually with skills, strategies, or processes) and student generated assessment (where students devise ways they will demonstrate competence on a particular topic at a particular level of proficiency).

1. **Performance tasks:** A *performance task* is an assessment that prompts students to research and analyze information, weigh evidence, and solve meaningful problems, allowing them to demonstrate their new learning. These can be used as common formative assessments, exit tickets, or as a problem to further develop a concept.

2. **Learning portfolios:** A *learning portfolio* is a dynamic assessment that allows students to demonstrate their learning. Learning portfolios can be traditional or digital, taking the form of a website, blog, or video documentary, just to name a few.

Performance Tasks

Performance tasks are learning experiences that allow students to evaluate their thinking through a solution pathway that resonates with their personal learning styles (such as visual, verbal, kinesthetic, and so on) and represents their current level of thinking about a concept. Teachers use performance tasks to determine what students know and what they are able to do relating to specific learning content; therefore, tasks must include a demonstration of learning and provide tangible evidence of learning.

Because performance tasks in mathematics build on previously learned skills and concepts and require students to synthesize learning in ways that makes sense in a particular context, this strategy makes for an effective formal assessment.

Figure 2.4 provides some examples of effective performance tasks at varying grade levels.

Elementary example:

Isabel sold some tubs of peanut butter cookie dough for a school fundraiser. Each tub costs $8. Isabel collected $32. How many tubs of cookie dough did Isabel sell? Show your work and write an equation. Explain how you solved the problem.

Middle school example:

Tony graphed $x < -4$. Show what the graph should look like. Also show a common mistake that Tony could have made and explain why.

High school example:

$$\frac{x + \dfrac{x}{2}}{\dfrac{x}{2} + \dfrac{3x}{2}}$$

Show why x does not equal zero. Justify your thinking.

Source: Adapted from Kanold, 2018.

Figure 2.4: Effective mathematics performance tasks.

With performance tasks, it's important for the teacher to plan for what he or she will be doing while students are engaged in the work. Teachers can consider the following questions.

- How will I present and then monitor student response to the task?
- How will I expect students to demonstrate proficiency of the learning target during in-class checks for understanding?
- How will I scaffold instruction for students who are stuck during the lesson or the lesson tasks (ask *assessing questions*)?
- How will I further learning for students who are ready to advance beyond the standard during class (ask *advancing questions*)?

Teachers should also consider what students should be doing during the task.

- How will students be actively engaged in each part of the lesson?
- What type of student discourse does this task require—whole group or small group?
- What mathematical thinking (reasoning, problem solving, or justification) are students developing during this task?

It is important to note that even though performance tasks make effective formal assessments, they are not simply bookends to a lesson. Performance tasks are authentic and therefore teachers should naturally integrate them into the learning context.

When instruction is focused on learning dispositions (reasoning, justifying, and problem solving)—how students behave when engaged in learning—performance task assessments are more integral to the learning environment because of the natural connection to instruction.

Learning Portfolios

Learning portfolios, traditionally made up of binders of student work or loose student work papers hung on a bulletin board, have taken a new shape within the digital age. Digital or web-based learning portfolios provide students with innovative ways of self-documenting and showcasing their learning through the creation of websites, videos, and blog posts. Learning portfolios not only provide an effective means of authentic assessment for teachers but they also give parents and other students a window into rigorous and relevant mathematics learning.

John Zubizarreta (2009) provides an effective framework for facilitation of student portfolios. It's important to ensure that students specifically align the content of learning portfolios to learning objectives and goals. The representation of student work or products is linked to the reflective component of the learning portfolio, and it is driven by purpose (real-world application of concepts) and audience (an authentic audience in addition to the teacher). The following list contains examples of pieces of work and student choice involved in portfolio construction.

- Daily mathematics reflections
- Exit tickets
- Mathematics think-alouds
- Mathematics projects
- Representations of good mathematics reasoning and problem-solving skills
- Proof of how the student went from confusion to understanding
- A sample of a "best fit" strategy in use with a student explanation of his or her best-fit strategy
- Performance tasks with reflections or corrections

- Proof of good mathematics collaboration, with justification of why it is considered good
- Something the student is really proud of, with explanation
- Collection of mathematics brainstorming and visual representations used to solve problems
- Collection of student-created explainer videos

Figure 2.5 shows a student reflection sheet for inclusion in a portfolio.

Final Mathematics Learning Portfolio Reflection

- What is something you are most proud of?
- What was the hardest concept you encountered and how did you conquer it? What is the evidence of your progression?
- What is something you would do differently next time?
- Choose a performance task that you're most proud of and talk about how you used the mathematical practices to create a solution.
- Looking over your work from the beginning of the learning portfolio to the end, what evidence shows growth either in your mathematics processes or concept understanding?
- How will you use your mathematics learning portfolio going forward? Did you find the process valuable?

Figure 2.5: Student mathematics learning portfolio ideas for all grade levels.

Visit go.SolutionTree.com/instruction for a free reproducible version of this figure.

Learning portfolios can also serve as a final product during an inquiry-based or project-based learning experience. Because this assessment strategy more closely emulates real-world work, students are highly motivated and become true curators of their own learning while also providing the teacher with data to use for appropriate feedback on current levels of learning.

Figure 2.6 presents the self-rating scale teachers can use for element 5, using formal assessments of individual students.

Score	Description
4: Innovating	I adapt behaviors and create new strategies for unique student needs and situations.
3: Applying	I use formal assessments of individual students to determine students' proficiency with specific content, and I monitor the extent to which students respond to assessment-guided feedback and instruction.
2: Developing	I use formal assessments of individual students to determine students' proficiency with specific content, but I do not monitor the effect on students.
1: Beginning	I use the strategies and behaviors associated with this element incorrectly or with parts missing.
0: Not Using	I am unaware of strategies and behaviors associated with this element.

Figure 2.6: Self-rating scale for element 5—Using formal assessments of individual students.

GUIDING QUESTIONS FOR CURRICULUM DESIGN

This overarching question can guide teachers when using assessments: *How will I design and administer assessments that help students understand how their test scores and grades relate to their status on the progression of knowledge they are expected to master?* Consider the following questions aligned to the elements in this chapter to guide your planning.

- **Element 4:** How will I informally assess the whole class?

_____

_____

_____

_____

_____

_____

_____

_____

_____

- **Element 5:** How will I formally assess individual students?

_____

_____

_____

_____

_____

_____

_____

_____

_____

_____

Summary

Using assessments involves two elements: (1) informal assessments of the whole class and (2) formal assessments of individual students. In the mathematics classroom, teachers can structure informal assessments using strategies like virtual exit slips, guided reciprocal peer questioning, and the RSQC2 process. They can use such formal assessments as performance tasks and online learning portfolios to help better understand student progress. In mathematics, we often think of assessments as dreaded and laborious tasks. With the strategies in this chapter, mathematics teachers can provide students with fun and motivating ways to show what they have learned and achieve deeper learning, while also understanding how students might be struggling and how to improve instruction or reteach to increase student success.

PART II
Content

CHAPTER 3

Conducting Direct Instruction Lessons

The third design area in *The New Art and Science of Teaching* framework involves addressing content in the classroom through direct instruction lessons. When mathematics content is new, students benefit greatly from direct instruction. Unfortunately, it is a common misperception that direct instruction refers to the presentation of new information in lecture format. This is far from the truth. As this chapter illustrates, mathematics teachers can deliver direct instruction in a variety of ways using specific strategies to facilitate students' understanding of the key parts of the new content and how these parts fit together.

Mathematics education researchers have demonstrated the importance of direct instruction. For example, Boaler (2002) finds that struggling students continue to struggle until the teacher intervenes and provides direct instruction. The work of Boaler (2015) shows that direct instruction is effective when teachers use models to encourage practice using real-life situations to teach students new concepts.

Direct instruction is most effective when teachers are introducing new concepts to students. It allows students to form connections between prior and new learning. For example, in the elementary classroom, students must be able to connect their understanding of whole numbers to the new concept of fractions. In the high school classroom, students must understand notations before learning the quadratic formula. Direct instruction facilitates processing of new content by supporting students to apply new concepts and skills to new contexts.

The elements in this third design area, conducting direct instruction lessons, include chunking content into appropriately sized segments (element 6), providing opportunities for students to process the content in each segment (element 7), and prompting students to record and represent content in a variety of modes (element 8). Here we describe how each element might manifest in a mathematics classroom to answer the question, *When mathematics content is new, how will I design and deliver direct instruction lessons that help students understand which parts of the content are important and how the parts fit together?*

Element 6: Chunking Content

Chunking content involves creating small, understandable increments of information or skills that students can hold in their working memory. In *The New Art and Science of Teaching* framework, Marzano (2017) identifies three specific strategies for chunking content.

1. Using preassessment data to plan for chunks
2. Presenting content in small, sequentially related sets
3. Allowing for processing time between chunks

Marzano (2017) advises that unlike strategies in most other elements, it is best to employ those listed for chunking sequentially. Here we describe how that might look in the mathematics classroom.

Using Preassessment Data to Plan for Chunks

First, teachers can consider using preassessment data to plan for chunks. This is about determining students' readiness for the new content—if they know enough about the content to be able to handle larger chunks, or if they require smaller chunks because they are less knowledgeable about the new content. In the mathematics classroom, a preassessment can be informal. For example, a preassessment about a strategy for multicolumn subtraction might simply be to present a problem to the entire class and ask students to describe how they would approach the task. If the vast majority of students seem to understand how to approach the problem, the teacher could conclude that presenting the process in two sets of steps would be sufficient, since students already seem to have a general sense of what to do. If students do not seem familiar with the process, the teacher would spend more time presenting and exemplifying individual steps. A preassessment could also be more structured and take the form of a hardcopy test that addresses the various levels of the proficiency scale.

For example, in an algebra 2 class, the teacher would present a problem to the entire class and ask students to describe how they would approach the task. The teacher would then ask students to identify key features of polynomial functions. Students might start with a graphing example of a linear function and two quadratic functions. Students will identify the key features—zeros, end behavior, maximum and minimum, and so on. Students will make connections to what they know about linear and quadratic functions as the class gets ready for the tasks of the lesson.

If the vast majority of students seem to understand how to approach the problem, the teacher could conclude that presenting the process from linear to quadratic would be sufficient since students already seem to have a general sense of what to do. If students do not seem familiar with the process, the teacher would spend more time presenting and exemplifying linear functions and how they connect to quadratic functions. A preassessment could also be more structured and take the form of a mathematics task that addresses the various levels of the proficiency scale.

Presenting Content in Small, Sequentially Related Sets

The second strategy refers to using the chunking process to present the learning. While presenting the content, the teacher should monitor student understanding. If students aren't grasping the new learning, the teacher must go back into the content before presenting a new chunk.

For example, in an elementary classroom, consider the teaching of fractions. When teachers first formally introduce students to fractions, they start to develop the idea of fractions by building on the concept of dividing a whole into equal parts. Before students divide the whole into parts, they begin with fractions with a numerator of 1. This is the first conceptual chunk of the lesson: identifying equal parts and taking one part. If a whole is partitioned into three equal parts, then each part is one-third of the whole. Additionally, to help students visually process concepts, teachers can introduce number lines.

At the intermediate level, students learning ratios must first understand the language that helps them recognize ratios, rates, and proportions. The chunking strategy here would focus on the terms *for every*, *for each*, *to*, and *per* and how they represent different but equivalent ways of identifying ratios and rates, which is foundational to understanding the structure of ratio tables. The next crucial chunk of information about ratios is the roles of multiplication and division operations.

At the secondary level, consider an algebra classroom. In traditional algebra instruction (including teaching the quadratic formula), students would be busy performing multiple drills on equations of erroneous values. This technique, however, hinders students' grasp of the underlying reasoning behind solving quadratic equations; thus, they don't have the freedom and cognition to choose the method that best suits the context. When chunking content, teachers must begin by reinforcing the conceptual chunk of factoring. Factoring can be complex (like trying to determine what ingredients went into a prepared dish of food) if students do not have a solid foundation; therefore, the teacher must determine the students who need some additional support with factoring. The next conceptual chunk would then be completing the square.

Allowing for Processing Time Between Chunks

The final strategy for chunking deals with providing structured time for students to interact about the content the teacher has presented. The teacher structures this processing time. For example, he or she organizes students into groups and gives each group member specific responsibilities.

We recommend that teachers use the scale in figure 3.1 to rate their current level of effectiveness in regard to chunking content.

Score	Description
4: Innovating	I adapt behaviors and create new strategies for unique student needs and situations.
3: Applying	I chunk content, and I monitor the extent to which my actions affect students.
2: Developing	I chunk content, but I do not monitor the effect on students.
1: Beginning	I use the strategies and behaviors associated with this element incorrectly or with parts missing.
0: Not Using	I am unaware of strategies and behaviors associated with this element.

Figure 3.1: Self-rating scale for element 6—Chunking content.

Element 7: Processing Content

Chunking content is only part of an effective framework for direct instruction. Teachers must also create opportunities for students to process the learning to help ensure that they can apply and build on it with the next concept. Processing content in the mathematics classroom involves giving students opportunities to think about each chunk of information the teacher provides before progressing to the next chunk.

The New Art and Science of Teaching framework identifies specific strategies for processing content, including perspective analysis, thinking hats, collaborative process, jigsaw cooperative learning, reciprocal teaching, concept attainment, think-pair-share, and scripted cooperative dyads (Marzano, 2017).

To continue the previous fraction example in the chunking section from the elementary classroom, as part of processing this conceptual chunk of learning, the teacher prompts students to work in collaborative groups to build fractions from unit fractions, seeing the numerator 2 in the fraction ⅔, saying that ⅔ is the value that occurs when combining ⅓ and ⅓ together.

In the intermediate example on ratios, the teacher assigns reciprocal teaching groups in which students teach each other how the processing step allows them to focus on the rows and columns of a ratio table as multiples (not additives) of each other. In the secondary example of solving the quadratic formula, students process content as they continually develop the understanding that solving equations is a reasoning process. The reasoning begins from the assumption that x is equal to some number that solves the equation and provides a list of possible values for x. When students possess an understanding that solving quadratic equations is a reasoning process of ordered steps they have memorized, students can organize the various methods for solving different problems holistically.

As Marzano (2017) writes, the goal of implementing these strategies is to observe positive behaviors in students, such as students actively interacting with the content, volunteering predictions, accurately explaining what they just learned, and voluntarily asking questions for clarification.

We recommend that teachers use the scale in figure 3.2 to rate their current level of effectiveness with processing content.

Score	Description
4: Innovating	I adapt behaviors and create new strategies for unique student needs and situations.
3: Applying	I engage students in processing content, and I monitor the extent to which my actions affect students.
2: Developing	I engage students in processing content, but I do not monitor the effect on students.
1: Beginning	I use the strategies and behaviors associated with this element incorrectly or with parts missing.
0: Not Using	I am unaware of strategies and behaviors associated with this element.

Figure 3.2: Self-rating scale for element 7—Processing content.

Element 8: Recording and Representing Content

Marzano (2017) describes this element as the process of students representing content through encoding, either linguistically (through language) or nonlinguistically (through pictures). Additionally, technology has given students the ability to use representations to make their thinking more visible. Following are some technology tools mathematics teachers can employ when asking students to record and represent content. These tools can also serve strategies such as implementing digital graphic organizers, summaries, pictorial notes, academic notebooks, and outlines or concept maps that *The New Art and Science of Teaching* framework identifies.

- **Flipgrid (https://flipgrid.com):** Flipgrid is a video discussion platform for educators, students, and families. When using this tool, students use the camera on their device to record their representation of the content. Students can draw or use custom stickers in their representation, and they can also link other files or media to verbalize their thinking on the concepts. For example, using this tool, grade 6 mathematics students might create a graphic organizer of the different mathematics topics and skills they have learned. Students save their responses on their grid (a repository of videos), and they can then go back and review if they are struggling with any concepts.

- **Kaizena (www.kaizena.com):** Kaizena is a feedback tool for use in Google Docs. Students construct responses about a mathematics concept using Kaizena. Then, using text or a voice recorder, the teacher communicates with students about their work and tracks their learning progress by viewing and comparing previous feedback from past constructive response prompts.
- **Recap (https://letsrecap.com):** Recap is a question-led chat tool that uses video. To support processing in between chunks, students record and submit questions to the teacher during independent practice. The teacher supports student questioning by providing question stems. For example, "What would happen if . . ." and "I understand this, but I'm still having difficulty with . . ." Additionally, students can submit questions with visual representations of their thinking.
- **Sketchboard (https://sketchboard.io):** Sketchboard is an online whiteboard. Students can create a visual representation (sketch) of the newly learned mathematics concept. The tool supports student processing by allowing them to represent ideas with a library of icons, or students can freehand their own representation. Additionally, during small-group instruction, the teacher may prompt students to collaborate on a sketch.
- **WeVideo (www.wevideo.com):** WeVideo is an online video editor. Students can create a video on mathematics concepts they just learned, beginning by creating a storyboard and script that contain not only mathematics content but real-world examples that are exciting and meaningful. They share their storyboard with other students for the purpose of receiving feedback within the video creation platform. They can share their videos in the classroom, on the learning management system, or on social media.

Tools change and evolve over time, therefore it's more important to home in on what students are doing and how they can represent content in various ways. Teachers must expect students to think with complexity and apply knowledge and skills to unpredictable situations, not just ask students to think with complexity or to extend knowledge and skills to solve a problem. Educators provide a framework or structure for thinking and learning, allowing students to solve problems in their own way and justify their thinking, all while providing opportunities for students to make their thinking visible.

Figure 3.3 presents the self-rating scale for recording and representing content.

Score	Description
4: Innovating	I adapt behaviors and create new strategies for unique student needs and situations.
3: Applying	I have students record and represent content, and I monitor the extent to which my actions affect students' performance.
2: Developing	I have students record and represent content, but I do not monitor the effect on students.
1: Beginning	I use the strategies and behaviors associated with this element incorrectly or with parts missing.
0: Not Using	I am unaware of strategies and behaviors associated with this element.

Figure 3.3: Self-rating scale for element 8—Recording and representing content.

GUIDING QUESTIONS FOR CURRICULUM DESIGN

This design question pertains to conducting direct instruction lessons: *When content is new, how will I design and deliver direct instruction lessons that help students understand which parts are important and how the parts fit together?* Consider the following questions aligned to the elements in this chapter to guide your planning.

- **Element 6:** How will I chunk the new content into short, digestible bites?

_____

_____

_____

_____

_____

_____

_____

- **Element 7:** How will I help students process the individual chunks and the content as a whole?

_____

_____

_____

_____

_____

_____

_____

_____

- **Element 8:** How will I help students record and represent their knowledge?

_____

_____

_____

_____

_____

_____

_____

_____

Summary

Conducting direct instruction lessons involves three elements: (1) chunking content, (2) processing content, and (3) recording and representing content. In the mathematics classroom, teachers should consider how to apply each of these elements to daily instructional practices. These strategies help students model mathematics, organize the new mathematics concepts and vocabulary, and support meaning-making for new concepts. It is important that students understand not just the mathematics vocabulary but also how to represent a concept (like fractions, groups, equations, and so on) visually and be able to provide multiple examples.

CHAPTER 4

Conducting Practicing and Deepening Lessons

Once students have grasped the important ideas and structure of new content, they need to deepen their understanding of concepts and develop fluency with new skills and processes. When planning instruction to practice and deepen students' knowledge of mathematics, it is important to make a distinction between two types of knowledge: (1) declarative and (2) procedural.

Procedural knowledge involves complex processes and the basic skills that are the components of the larger processes. Certainly, solving different types of mathematics problems involves processes, and the operations of adding, subtracting, multiplying, and dividing involve skills. *Declarative knowledge* is informational in nature. It involves details such as facts and terminology, but also, more broadly, it involves generalizations, principles, and concepts. Some mathematics content such as rational and irrational numbers involves important terminology and facts in addition to important generalizations, principles, and concepts.

To a certain extent, mathematics teachers must determine whether they wish to emphasize the important mathematics declarative knowledge, procedural knowledge, or both when they design practicing and deepening lessons.

This is the focus of the fourth design area in *The New Art and Science of Teaching* framework—to support such practice and deepening. To do so, teachers can use structured practice sessions (element 9), help students examine similarities and differences in content (element 10), and prompt students to investigate possible errors in reasoning relative to specific content (element 11). Here we describe how each element of this design area might manifest in a mathematics classroom.

Element 9: Using Structured Practice Sessions

Practice and fluency are important facets of effective teaching in mathematics, but they are commonly misunderstood. Mathematics content always contains a skill, strategy, or process, and therefore the teacher must provide students with well-structured opportunities to practice to develop their learning. In *The New Art and Science of Teaching* framework (Marzano, 2017) identifies this strategy for element 9 as guided practice. Practice is more than repetition; it involves students gradually learning and then shaping the steps of a process. Teachers must thoughtfully plan and facilitate the process.

Mathematics standards call for students to possess mathematics fluency. Practice helps develop fluency. Fluency practice is another strategy Marzano identifies in his framework for element 9. This fluency is often confused with rote memorization. Catherine Fosnot and Maarten Dolk (2001) define *fluency* as knowing how a number can be composed and decomposed and using that information to be flexible and efficient with solving problems.

In a compelling study, researchers Gray and Tall (1994) studied students, aged seven to thirteen, as they solved number problems. The students in the study were identified by their teachers as being low, middle, or high achievers. The researchers found a significant difference between the low- and high-achieving students; the high-achieving students used flexibility (or number sense), while the low-achieving students did not. For example, consider the problem 15 + 4. High achievers thought through the problem in this way: "Two 5s get you 10, and 5 + 4 = 9, so 10 + 9 = 19." No low-achieving students used such number sense to solve the problem. Another example of the difference in thinking appeared during subtraction. For example, in the problem 21 – 16, low-achieving students counted backward, starting at 21, and counting down to 20, 19, 18, and so forth. The high-achieving students changed the problem to 20–15, easily determining the answer to be 5. The-low achieving students were dealing with a higher cognitive load than the high-achieving students. The researchers conclude that low achievers struggle not because they know less but because they don't use numbers flexibly. Boaler (2009) states these students have been set on the wrong path, often from an early age, of trying to memorize methods instead of interacting with numbers flexibly. She concludes the best way to develop fluency with numbers is to develop number sense and to work with numbers in different ways, not to blindly memorize without number sense.

Following are some fluency practice approaches to apply this strategy in mathematics classrooms.

- **Number talks (all levels):** Researchers Cathy Humphreys and Ruth Parker (2015) have created strategies that help teachers support students in investigating mathematical relationships and ideas through "number talks." Their research reveals that the best mathematics classrooms are those in which students learn number facts and number sense through engaging activities that focus on mathematical understanding rather than rote memorization. Students reason aloud with mathematics when teachers prompt them in an organized way. The following examples of number talk stems can facilitate these conversations.
  - "Show me how you divide this triangle into smaller triangles."
  - "Can you show me why you believe this is correct?"
  - "Please describe your method clearly."
  - "Would anyone do it another way?"
  - "Show me another strategy to solve this algebra problem."
  - "How do you know this is correct? Please describe your method clearly."
  - "Would someone else do it another way?"
- **Number alter ego (elementary):** With this strategy, the teacher helps students find as many different ways as possible for representing the number 23, such as 30 – 7 or 10 + 10 + 3. (These different equations are alter egos for 23.) The teacher asks students to work in groups to come up with alter egos, encouraging them to use strategies like skip-counting by fives or decomposing numbers. Students might construct responses like "two tens and three ones." This strategy supports students' ability to create coherent representations of numbers, reason through mathematics, and develop fluency.

- **Should I invest? (intermediate):** In this strategy, the teacher asks students to determine the amount of money they will make by investing in a particular stock. They do this using multiplication of interest rates. Students all receive the same hypothetical amount to start with: $100. Then, they research stock prices and their respective returns. With a partner, they choose the stocks they want to invest in and their strategies, detailing how they reasoned through the mathematics of determining rate of return. Consistently working the multiplication of decimals and reasoning out loud builds number fluency to support high-level thinking.

- **Comparing phones (secondary):** Jon R. Star and Bethany Rittle-Johnson (2009) suggest a comparison strategy for algebra students. In the activity, students are interested in purchasing a smartphone and want to make the best choice. They narrow down their options to two phones. One way to do this is to view the information about each phone separately, reading the specifications, reviews, and price information for each phone individually. However, reading the long lists of dozens of features associated with each phone's camera alone would make it very difficult for students to notice which features of the phones are similar and which features are different. Instead, they decide to compare the same information by viewing the features of the two phones at the same time, side by side. A quick glance at a comparison chart, which students could develop, allows students to easily distinguish whether the phones are the same or different for important features. Comparing the phones side by side helps them easily identify the salient similarities and differences. After students draw conclusions from this activity, the teacher places a side-by-side comparison of two approaches to solving a linear equation on the whiteboard. (See figure 4.1.)

The teacher then facilitates a discussion in which students compare the two solution paths. Students then receive another problem and generate an alternative solution path and share their strategy with a partner.

$3(x + 1) = 15$	$3(x + 1) = 15$
$3x + 3 = 15$	$x + 1 = 5$
$3x = 12$	$x = 4$
$x = 4$	

Figure 4.1: Side-by-side comparison of two equations.

Figure 4.2 presents the self-rating scale to guide teachers in addressing element 9, using structured practice sessions.

Score	Description
4: Innovating	I adapt behaviors and create new strategies for unique student needs and situations.
3: Applying	I use structured practice sessions, and I monitor the extent to which my actions affect students.
2: Developing	I use structured practice sessions, but I do not monitor the effect on students.
1: Beginning	I use the strategies and behaviors associated with this element incorrectly or with parts missing.
0: Not Using	I am unaware of strategies and behaviors associated with this element.

Figure 4.2: Self-rating scale for element 9—Using structured practice sessions.

Element 10: Examining Similarities and Differences

This element helps students deepen their understanding by examining how items are alike and not alike. Strategies within this element apply to both declarative and procedural knowledge. Consider the concepts of measuring the area of a rectangle in grade 3 and solving quadratic equations in algebra 2, which are declarative in nature. Teachers might ask students to identify and articulate characteristics that are common to both concepts and unique to each concept. This would most likely deepen their understanding of both. The same is true for procedural knowledge when students are first learning it. When students are learning the procedure as information, it is useful to have them examine the similarities and differences between the procedure they are newly learning and a procedure they have already learned. For example, if a teacher is introducing students to the procedure for multicolumn subtraction, it would be useful to have them examine its similarities and differences with the procedure of multicolumn addition, which they learned previously.

Marzano (2018) identifies several strategies for examining similarities and differences. In the mathematics classroom, students can create a comparison matrix. Have students identify strong and not-strong-yet work, and then discuss as a class how to make each sample stronger. Or when giving students their work back, ask them to make their solutions stronger and clearer using a comparison matrix.

To use visual comparisons, break students into groups. Provide each group with a different image. Ask the groups to create mathematical questions for the image. Then ask groups to switch papers and solve the other group's questions using the image.

To use sentence-stem analogies, give students stems that contain vocabulary words pertinent to the mathematics concepts the class is exploring, such as *parts, graphing, polygon, polynomial,* and so on. Ask students to finish the sentence with words they may need to address the concept or task, such as *factoring, measure, volume, height, circumference, radius,* and so on). Collect the words students choose, display them, and encourage students to think about how they would solve upcoming tasks using the words they came up with.

Figure 4.3 presents the self-rating scale for examining similarities and differences.

Score	Description
4: Innovating	I adapt behaviors and create new strategies for unique student needs and situations.
3: Applying	I engage students in examining similarities and differences, and I monitor the extent to which students deepen their knowledge.
2: Developing	I engage students in examining similarities and differences, but I do not monitor the effect on students.
1: Beginning	I use the strategies and behaviors associated with this element incorrectly or with parts missing.
0: Not Using	I am unaware of strategies and behaviors associated with this element.

Figure 4.3: Self-rating scale for element 10—Examining similarities and differences.

Element 11: Examining Errors in Reasoning

Brain research reveals that examining errors in reasoning helps deepen students' learning of content. Psychologist Jason S. Moser (2011) discovered that errors contribute to brain growth. In his study, he explains that when people make errors, the brain has two potential responses: error-related negativity (ERN) and error positivity (PE). During an ERN response, there is increased electrical activity when the brain experiences conflict between a correct response and an error. The PE response occurs in the brain when we are conscious of the error. The results of this study show that growth mindset is associated with an enhanced PE amplitude reflecting the detection and conscious attention to the errors and with improved performance subsequently following the making of errors.

Thus, making mistakes in mathematics should be an integral part of classroom activity as it not only encourages healthy motivation for learning but also contributes to deeper learning experiences through neural activity.

Following are several instructional tools that support K–12 students in leveraging errors in their reasoning to grow in their knowledge of mathematics. These tools support students in the strategies of identifying errors in misinformation, practicing identifying errors in logic, anticipating errors, and identifying errors.

- **Reasoning aloud:** This strategy is similar to a think-aloud, except that the focus is not on explicitly providing step-by-step directions on how to do something; rather, the focus is on thinking processes. The purpose of reasoning aloud is not to illuminate that there is one way, or only one right way, or the perfect way of doing something. It's also not to point out careless mistakes. This strategy is meant to identify erroneous reasoning (thinking processes). The teacher reasons out loud through a mathematics problem and purposefully includes natural errors in thought process.

  For example, an algebra teacher might reason aloud when evaluating $2(6x - 12)$ in the following way.

  - *Teacher:* "This is straightforward. I just multiply 2 by the number with the exponent. My new expression is $12x - 12$. Am I reasoning through this correctly?"
  - *Student:* "Wait, the coefficient means that the group is doubled? You didn't double the 12."
  - *Teacher:* "Oh, yes! Thank you for the reminder about the distributive property. Just as I've learned with the distributive property, I can break numbers apart (into addends) and multiply by the same factor. Since we need two groups of $6x - 12$. I know $6 \times 2 = 12$. And I also have to multiply 12 by the same factor as well. So, my expression is $12x - 24$."

- **Grouping patterns in errors:** This strategy asks students to make their thinking visible as they solve a problem. Typically, this would involve students showing visual representations of the problem or a narrative about how they solved the problem. This is different, however. The teacher collects a sampling of the problems (this can be done quickly through a collaboratively shared document). Then he or she asks students to collectively agree on the correct response. Students group the solutions based not on the correct response but instead based on the solution path. For example, if students are solving a two-digit addition problem, some students might use the break-apart method to take full advantage of the distributive property. Some students may use the traditional vertical addition method. Others may choose to use a number line. In this example, students would have grouped solutions into three groups: (1) break apart, (2) vertical addition, and (3) number line. The class would then analyze the solution paths to determine which path yielded the most correct answers. Additionally, they would analyze any consistent errors in a particular strategy. For example, they would note if some students went the negative direction on the number line instead of the positive direction.

- **Peer reviewing:** When using peer reviewing, teachers ask students to exchange their solutions with classmates. The classmates check for errors in reasoning and mistakes. Reviewers circle mistakes and make comments on erroneous reasoning. Using digital tools—a collaborative, shared digital document, for example—aids in making this a seamless process.

Figure 4.4 contains the self-rating scale for element 11, examining errors in reasoning.

Score	Description
4: Innovating	I adapt behaviors and create new strategies for unique student needs and situations.
3: Applying	When content is informational, I engage students in activities that require them to examine their own reasoning or the logic of information as presented to them, and I monitor the extent to which students are deepening their knowledge.
2: Developing	When content is informational, I engage students in activities that require them to examine their own reasoning or the logic of information as presented to them, but I do not monitor the effect on students.
1: Beginning	I use the strategies and behaviors associated with this element incorrectly or with parts missing.
0: Not Using	I am unaware of strategies and behaviors associated with this element.

Figure 4.4: Self-rating scale for element 11—Examining errors in reasoning.

GUIDING QUESTIONS FOR CURRICULUM DESIGN

This design question focuses on practicing and deepening lessons: *After presenting content, how will I design and deliver lessons that help students deepen their understanding and develop fluency in skills and processes?* Consider the following questions aligned to the elements in this chapter to guide your planning.

- **Element 9:** How will I help students engage in structured practice?

_____

_____

_____

_____

_____

_____

_____

_____

_____

_____

_____

_____

- **Element 10:** How will I help students examine similarities and differences?

_____

_____

_____

_____

_____

_____

_____

_____

_____

_____

- **Element 11:** How will I help students examine errors in reasoning?

_____

_____

_____

_____

_____

_____

_____

_____

_____

_____

_____

Summary

Unfortunately, many mathematics teachers focus on fluency and practice in ways that give students the impression that practice, drills, tips, and tricks are the focus of solving mathematics problems. Ideally, mathematics practice and fluency should illuminate the flexible nature of numbers and the different mathematical contexts that exist. The three elements this chapter presented—(1) structured practice sessions, (2) examining similarities and differences, and (3) examining errors in reasoning—reinforce the importance of practice along with deep understanding of numbers and the relationships among them.

CHAPTER 5

Conducting Knowledge Application Lessons

Knowledge application lessons provide opportunities for students to use what they have learned in unique situations—to go beyond classroom learning and devise solutions in real-world scenarios. This design area is vital to effective mathematics instruction if students are to develop deeper learning. In many mathematics classrooms, teachers struggle to get away from using the bulk of classroom time and energy on solving equations, practicing operations, and memorizing algorithms. To build deeper learning, teachers must focus on developing skills like problem solving and critical thinking by employing real-life scenarios in which students use the tools of mathematics (equations, algorithms, apps, calculators, and so on) as a means of supporting their application of knowledge.

Three elements support knowledge application tasks. Students engage in cognitively complex tasks (element 12) that generate new awareness about the mathematics content they have learned. Teachers provide resources and guidance (element 13) to help students generate and defend claims (element 14).

Element 12: Engaging Students in Cognitively Complex Tasks

Cognitively complex mathematical tasks help reveal how students reason through mathematics. They also allow students to critique and revise their work while providing an engaging way to present their final product to a relevant audience.

Before we discuss strategies for implementing cognitively complex tasks in the mathematics classroom, it's necessary to understand the importance of such tasks and note their criteria. Introducing a complex task influences the learning experience for the students and impacts what the teacher is able to assess during the learning experience. Teachers must create a meaningful and engaging task focused on student learning goals and based on mathematics standards and other content-based standards (such as English language arts, science, social studies, and so on). Additionally, tasks should build skills such as critical thinking, creativity, citizenship, problem-solving ability, communication, collaboration, and self-management.

In *The New Art and Science of Teaching* framework, Marzano (2017) identifies experimental inquiry tasks, problem-solving tasks, decision-making tasks, and investigative tasks as strategies for element 12. Mathematics teachers can use project-based learning (PBL) and the Rigor Relevance Framework as tools to support such strategies.

Project-Based Learning

Project-based learning provides experiences through which students gain knowledge and skills by working for an extended period of time to investigate and respond to an authentic, engaging, and complex questions, problems, or challenges. PBL experiences also allow students to strengthen the skills they need for life (the skills of critical thinking, creativity, problem solving, and so on) and to engage in learning that's fun and relevant. The Buck Institute for Education (2018), one of the leading voices in PBL, provides support and examples to help teachers plan for engaging projects that constitute complex tasks.

Figure 5.1 presents a project idea for grade 5 that integrates media, real-life skills, and mathematical content into a collaborative and engaging project.

Scenario

Students, in the role of financial advisors, are challenged to find the best use of $25.00 so that the funds make the most impact in a community. They will select a project from the organization Kiva, an international nonprofit with a mission to connect people through microlending to alleviate poverty, to provide with a $25.00 microloan. To help students determine the best use of the funds, they will conduct interviews with a banker to learn how lending works and with investors to learn about the projects they are passionate about. Students will also factor in repayment schedules, as well as delinquency and default rates, for the project and microlender. Students, teachers, and community members will be the investors. Students will be in charge of taking the funds and investing them into Kiva so the borrowers can begin their project. The end product is a presentation (student-created video, PowerPoint, narrative, or other medium) that students share with the investors, as well as the school and local community, to get their Kiva projects fully funded.

Learning Targets or Standards

Students can use operations with decimals to solve a real-world problem and explain their reasoning through models. (5.NBT.B.)

Present an opinion, sequencing ideas logically and using appropriate facts and relevant descriptive details to support main ideas. (SL.5.4)

Product

Students first collaboratively develop a plan for their presentation by creating a storyboard. In this scenario, students decide to create a video that includes media (photos, music, and so on) and interview clips from the borrower's community. Students choose whom they interview and determine how to sequence the story to generate the most impact. The video includes the students' own thoughts and opinions predicting future success of the community. It also explains why they believe this project will make the biggest impact on the community.

Source for standards: National Governors Association Center for Best Practices & Council of Chief State School Officers, 2010.
Source: Adapted from Buck Institute for Education, 2018.

Figure 5.1: Project-based learning project for grade 5 mathematics.

Other examples include elementary students investigating the environmental impact of a certain pollutant in a natural forest, such as empty water bottles dumped in a stream. Students use the four operations to solve word problems involving distance, intervals of time, liquid volumes, masses of objects, and money.

Secondary students could be challenged to design a new container (such as a purse, backpack, garbage can, and so on) based on mathematical models (such as polynomial functions).

The Rigor Relevance Framework

A tool that can ensure tasks are cognitively complex is the Rigor Relevance Framework, created by the International Center for Leadership in Education (2018), which builds on Bloom's taxonomy (see figure 5.2).

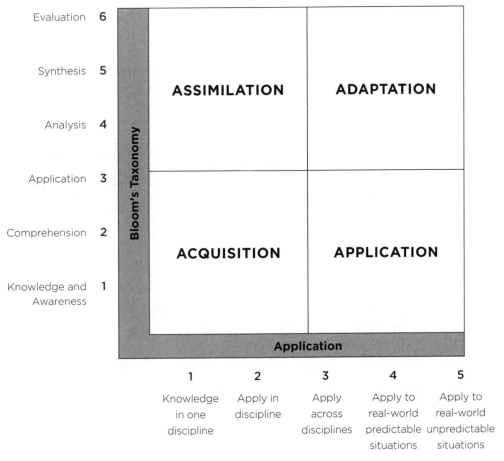

Source: Adapted from ICLE, 2018.

Figure 5.2: The Rigor Relevance Framework.

The vertical axis represents the six levels adapted from Bloom: (1) evaluation, (2) synthesis, (3) analysis, (4) application, (5) comprehension, and (6) knowledge and awareness.

The horizontal axis in the application model demonstrates in specific detail methods by which teachers can put knowledge to use in meaningful ways.

- Gain knowledge in one discipline.
- Apply knowledge in discipline.
- Apply knowledge across disciplines.
- Apply knowledge to real-world, predictable situations.
- Apply knowledge to real-world, unpredictable situations.

Acquisition represents the lowest degree of effectiveness, where students simply recall and possess a basic understanding of knowledge. Adaptation represents the highest degree of effectiveness, where knowledge and skills are used to create something new to solve complex, real-world problems that students care about.

Adaptation challenges students to think with complexity as they evaluate solutions to a problem. They must analyze multiple sources of data from either the task itself or from research they collected while engaging with the task. They then create a deliverable using an iterative process that involves multiple steps, each with its own demands. Applying the Rigor Relevance Framework turns a basic algebra concept of solving linear equations into a potential project of students giving recommendations to the city on how to use a newly acquired plot of land, applying their knowledge and skills on matrices and linear equations.

Figure 5.3 contains the self-rating scale for element 12, engaging students in cognitively complex tasks.

Score	Description
4: Innovating	I adapt behaviors and create new strategies for unique student needs and situations.
3: Applying	I engage students in cognitively complex tasks, and I monitor the extent to which my actions affect students.
2: Developing	I engage students in cognitively complex tasks, but I do not monitor the effect on students.
1: Beginning	I use the strategies and behaviors associated with this element incorrectly or with parts missing.
0: Not Using	I am unaware of strategies and behaviors associated with this element.

Figure 5.3: Self-rating scale for element 12—Engaging students in cognitively complex tasks.

Element 13: Providing Resources and Guidance

Engaging in cognitively complex tasks is not easy; therefore, teachers must provide students with resources and guidance. In the mathematics classroom, the teacher's role shifts from providing new content (direct instruction) or orchestrating the ways students are analyzing content (practicing and deepening lessons) to providing students with support as they apply knowledge to cognitively complex tasks. Teacher guidance should be simple yet structured enough to prompt students to reflect on their learning when they would not have otherwise.

One strategy *The New Art and Science of Teaching* framework identifies for this element is providing resources. Concept maps are an effective resource in the mathematics classroom to support students in discovering how they think, which will, in turn, support them in complex cognitive tasks. Researchers Ron Ritchhart, Terri Turner, and Linor Hadar (2009) study the effect of using concept maps to uncover student thinking. They conclude that students' engagement in thinking is dependent on their understanding and beliefs about how thinking happens. The very act of unpacking what it means to think can help students become more self-directed learners and better thinkers. Concept maps provide a window into students' attitude toward learning and enable them to develop an appreciation of the complexities of thinking and learning.

Ron Ritchhart, Mark Church, and Karin Morrison (2011) develop a type of concept map called an understanding map that students can use to evaluate their own understanding of a big idea or concept associated with a complex cognitive task. Students and teachers can continually reference their understanding map as their understanding changes and evolves. Figure 5.4 shows a template for an understanding map.

Consider Different Viewpoints	Reason With Evidence	Make Connections
What's another angle on this?	Why do you think so?	How does this fit?

UNDERSTANDING

Describe What's There	Build Explanations	Capture the Heart and Form Conclusions
What do you see and notice?	What's really going on here?	What's at the core or center of this?

Source: Ritchhart, Church, & Morrison, 2011.

Figure 5.4: Understanding map.

*Visit **go.SolutionTree.com/instruction** for a free reproducible version of this figure.*

As a mathematics instructor, it's important to understand your role while students are working in groups. What behaviors do you reinforce? How do you provide feedback if students are stuck? How do your teams know how to behave (what are the norms)? These questions can be answered through an effective circulation around the room, another strategy in *The New Art and Science of Teaching* framework:

- Extensively walk the room and observe student work.
- Listen to student and group conversations.
- Redirect student and small-group questions back to the whole group.
- Observe and praise success and encourage those who are not working with comments such as, "Great thinking!" "Wonderful processing skills!"
- Affirm work that is done well, and tell students to share their work with someone who is struggling with the problem.
- Positively reinforce and encourage students who are helping others.
- Keep track of time and remind students with a verbal command such as, "You have two minutes remaining."

Other ideas to support successful small-group learning prior to circulating the room include the following.

- To help support teams, use a student self-assessment to gather information from teams about individual student participation.
- Do timed team challenges for friendly competition in class, which adds energy—especially on days when students may seem sluggish.

We depict the self-reflection scale for element 13, providing resources and guidance, in figure 5.5 (page 52).

Score	Description
4: Innovating	I adapt behaviors and create new strategies for unique student needs and situations.
3: Applying	I provide resources and guidance, and I monitor the extent to which my actions affect students' performance.
2: Developing	I provide resources and guidance, but I do not monitor the effect on students.
1: Beginning	I use the strategies and behaviors associated with this element incorrectly or with parts missing.
0: Not Using	I am unaware of strategies and behaviors associated with this element.

Figure 5.5: Self-rating scale for element 13—Providing resources and guidance.

Element 14: Generating and Defending Claims

Generating and defending claims involves a high level of complexity in thinking. Thus, teachers should provide students with scaffolding with which they can develop their ideas and insights, building to higher levels of cognition. When generating and defending claims in mathematics, students grapple with the process—the sequence of how to defend their claim (the order in which the claim unfolds), the variety of evidence to incorporate, and how to identify mathematical concepts that connect strongly to their defense of the claim.

Mathematics teachers must be equipped to provide guidance so that students can effectively demonstrate this level of cognition. At the highest levels of defending claims, the teacher asks students to contrast strategies. Students defend and justify their answers with little prompting from the teacher. The tool in figure 5.6, the Four Cs to Defending Claims (care, criteria, critical, claim), is designed to help students more effectively consider how they will generate and defend their claims. This tool supports teachers in implementing the strategies Marzano (2017) notes in *The New Art and Science of Teaching* framework for generating and defending claims: introducing the concept of claim and support, presenting the formal structure of claims and support, generating claims, providing grounds and backing, and formally presenting claims. Figure 5.7 shows a completed example of the tool.

Why do I and others care?
Imagine the application of the mathematics concept to the real world or create a drawing on paper. Does it elicit emotion? Is it meaningful to you personally? Is it exciting?
Guiding question: Why must I defend this claim? What problem am I solving? What do I ultimately want to express?
What are your criteria?
Identify the criteria that you will use to align, measure, and critically assess your claim.
Guiding question: How will I know when I've successfully defended my claim?
What critical elements are required?
Identify the essential elements that, when brought together, will create the optimal sequence to best visibly express the ideals of the claim I'm making.
Guiding question: How well do these elements connect to successful criteria?
What constraints bind this claim?
Identify constraints that are a part of this claim. Evaluate the materials, resources, and time you have.
Guiding question: How will I leverage constraints to most effectively defend my claim?

Figure 5.6: The Four Cs to Defending Claims.

*Visit **go.SolutionTree.com/instruction** for a free reproducible version of this figure.*

Why do I and others care?

Imagine the application of the mathematics concept to the real world or draw it on paper. Does it elicit emotion? Is it meaningful to you personally? Is it exciting?

Guiding question: Why must I defend this claim? What problem am I solving? What do I ultimately want to express?

In math, we are working on a project to help investors decide on the best investment. I need to apply my understanding of multiplying percentages, which is converted to a decimal number, in this project. I will evaluate which community project is the most compelling based on the interests of my investors or what I believe their interests are. In my defense, I must have an understanding of how loans work. Ultimately, I want to give investors the peace of mind that their money is going to a meaningful cause.

What are your criteria?

Identify the criteria that you will use to align, measure, and critically assess your claim.

Guiding question: How will I know when I've successfully defended my claim?

During my defense and afterward, I will allow for questions. The kinds of questions my audience asks will give me the information I need to determine if I've effectively defended my claim. If I see evidence that the questions are not at the level of what I hoped to convey, I'll communicate in a different way to better convey my claim.

What critical elements are required?

Identify the essential elements that, when brought together, will create the optimal sequence to best visibly express the ideals of the claim I'm making.

Guiding question: How well do these elements connect to successful criteria?

The elements in the order of how I will defend my claim are as follows: purpose of the project, information about the community, the borrower's story, math behind lending, and a call to action.

What constraints bind this claim?

Identify constraints that are a part of this claim. Evaluate the materials, resources, and time you have.

Guiding question: How will I leverage constraints to most effectively defend my claim?

The community I've found to lend to on Kiva is culturally different and on another continent. Although I'm excited about all of the new things I'm learning about this community, language and communication can be a barrier. Also, I want to ensure I understand interest rates and percentages well so that I can confidently defend my claim.

Figure 5.7: Student example of the four Cs to defending claims.

Defending a claim can be daunting, as it entails more than just expressing why one chooses a particular idea. This tool provides a medium for enabling inspiration to flourish and provides student self-assessment opportunities. It's important that students are able to assess their own learning and see the relevance of how the work connects with the learning goals.

The ultimate goal of cognitively complex tasks is to give students the ability to generate and defend claims. Figure 5.8 contains the self-rating scale for element 14, generating and defending claims.

Score	Description
4: Innovating	I adapt behaviors and create new strategies for unique student needs and situations.
3: Applying	I engage students in activities that require them to generate and defend their own claims, and I monitor the extent to which students are applying their knowledge.
2: Developing	I engage students in activities that require them to generate and defend their own claims, but I do not monitor the effect on students.
1: Beginning	I use the strategies and behaviors associated with this element incorrectly or with parts missing.
0: Not Using	I am unaware of strategies and behaviors associated with this element.

Figure 5.8: Self-rating scale for element 14—Generating and defending claims.

To conduct knowledge application lessons, this is the design question to consider: *After presenting content, how will I design and deliver lessons that help students generate and defend claims through knowledge application?* Consider the following questions aligned to the elements in this chapter to guide your planning.

GUIDING QUESTIONS FOR CURRICULUM DESIGN

- **Element 12:** How will I engage students in cognitively complex tasks?

_____

_____

_____

_____

_____

_____

_____

- **Element 13:** How will I provide resources and guidance?

_____

_____

_____

_____

_____

_____

_____

_____

_____

- **Element 14:** How will I help students generate and defend claims?

_____

_____

_____

_____

_____

_____

_____

_____

Summary

Conducting knowledge application lessons involves three elements: (1) engaging students in cognitively complex tasks, (2) providing resources and guidance, and (3) generating and defending claims. In the mathematics classroom, cognitively complex tasks usually require students to apply prior knowledge; think non-algorithmically; and explore and understand the nature of mathematical concepts, processes, or relationships. They require considerable cognitive effort and may involve some level of anxiety for the student due to the unpredictable nature of the required solution process.

Tasks form the basis for student opportunities to learn what mathematics is and how one does mathematics. Teachers can scaffold these encounters by providing tools such as understanding maps to help students focus their analyses. Finally, because cognitively complex tasks typically culminate in generating and defending claims, they give students valuable experience with critical argumentation skills.

CHAPTER 6

Using Strategies That Appear in All Types of Lessons

Chapters 3, 4, and 5 describe specific types of lessons—direct instruction lessons, practicing and deepening lessons, and knowledge application lessons—each with unique purposes and strategies. This chapter focuses on elements and strategies that teacher can use in all three of these types of lessons. The combined purpose of the strategies is to help students continually integrate new knowledge with old knowledge and revise their understanding of the content accordingly. This should be a constant focus in the mathematics classroom—a continual loop in which teachers integrate content review with new learning. To this extent, we consider the strategies in this design area the tools with which students construct their own unique meaning for mathematics content.

The New Art and Science of Teaching framework identifies the following elements that involve strategies that teachers can use in all types of lessons: previewing strategies (element 15), highlighting critical information (element 16), reviewing content (element 17), revising content (element 18), reflecting on learning (element 19), assigning purposeful homework (element 20), elaborating on information (element 21), and organizing students to interact (element 22).

Element 15: Previewing Strategies

When teachers ask students to perform an activity or complete a task, they often simply set them loose. Students might start by conducting research, or making plans, or talking to their friends to get other opinions. While this is all appropriate, it lacks an important first step. Teachers should support students by first previewing content in meaningful ways before students dive into an activity. Before asking students to start solving or creating, teachers should provide the context for the work. What problem are students solving and why must they be the ones to solve it?

Previewing strategies give students a sneak peek at the content the teacher is about to address in order to activate students' background knowledge relative to it. Following is a list of strategies.

In addition, mathematics teachers can use the strategies Marzano (2017) suggests as part of *The New Art and Science of Teaching* framework.

- **Informational hooks:** This strategy uses activities to inspire interest in the content of an upcoming lesson. Such activities could include anecdotes, attention-grabbing media, video clips, or other items that spark student interest. Mathematics teachers might include games or contests to pique student interest. For example, a lesson in geometry might begin with a historical discussion of how shapes were named. A lesson in probability could start with a fun dice game.
- **Bell ringers:** As their name implies, bell ringers are activities at the very beginning of a class period that students are to engage in as soon as, or even before, the bell rings. For example, a teacher might have his or her students answer a brief question written on the board.
- **Anticipation guides:** Before presenting new content, the teacher has students respond to a series of statements that relate to upcoming information. After students respond to the statements, the teacher leads the class in a discussion about how students responded.
- **What do you think you know?** The teacher asks students to individually write down what they already know about an upcoming topic. After each student has created an individual list, the teacher asks students to pair up and discuss their previous knowledge and ideas. Finally, each pair shares its list, and the teacher creates a whole-class list of what students already know about upcoming content.

In mathematics, inquiry-based experiences are typically meant to encourage students to ask better questions in order to think more critically about a concept. But teachers can also use inquiry to harness student imagination and curiosity.

The creativity-assisted inquiry tool in figure 6.1 can help students ask better questions to guide them in the creation process while solving a cognitively complex problem. Additionally, it supports students in building on prior knowledge as they apply previous learning to more complex knowledge and skills.

Launch: Your teacher has shared some information with you that is intriguing. You already have some initial questions. What are they?

1.

2.

3.

4.

5.

Imagine: Review the questions you wrote. Choose the question that is most intriguing to you. Build on that question by letting your curiosity run wild. Use the prompts that follow to tap into your natural inquisitiveness.

- Create a metaphor that represents the concept in the question you chose.
- Share your metaphor with a classmate and ask him or her to build on your metaphor.
- Suppose that this concept played out in a different time or place; what would change?
- What was the preconcept, prestory, or backstory of this concept?

Create: Choose the prompt that is most intriguing to you and articulate your thinking (through storytelling) by creating a video, presentation, narrative brief, or other product.

Reflect: How did your thinking change from the first time you were introduced to the concept to after you created your product?

Figure 6.1: Creativity-assisted inquiry tool.

Visit go.SolutionTree.com/instruction for a free reproducible version of this figure.

Previewing helps students activate prior knowledge so that they might make connections to new knowledge. Figure 6.2 depicts the self-reflection scale for previewing strategies.

Score	Description
4: Innovating	I adapt behaviors and create new strategies for unique student needs and situations.
3: Applying	I engage students in learning activities that require them to preview and link new knowledge to what we have already addressed, and I monitor the extent to which students are making linkages.
2: Developing	I engage students in learning activities that require them to preview and link new knowledge to what we have already addressed, but I do not monitor the effect on students.
1: Beginning	I use the strategies and behaviors associated with this element incorrectly or with parts missing.
0: Not Using	I am unaware of strategies and behaviors associated with this element.

Figure 6.2: Self-rating scale for element 15—Previewing strategies.

Element 16: Highlighting Critical Information

Strategies for highlighting critical information involve the teacher pointing out what is important and what is less important in information he or she addresses in class. Teachers need to use these strategies because students receive a vast amount of incoming information during a single class period. Students hear what the teacher presents. They hear what other students say about the content. They read about the content, and they see diagrams of the content and demonstrations of problem solving. Not all of this information is equally important.

One way mathematics teachers can highlight critical information is to provide advance organizers. A foldable is a tool students can use to organize vocabulary for an upcoming mathematics unit. Most foldables require one sheet of paper that students fold or cut to creatively organize words, definitions, and examples. Figure 6.3 shows an example of a foldable for mathematics.

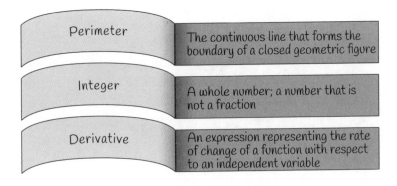

Figure 6.3: Example of a foldable for highlighting critical information.

Some of the strategies Marzano (2017) identifies in *The New Art and Science of Teaching* framework might seem to not be applicable in the mathematics classroom when in actuality these strategies go far in keeping student interest and highlighting important information.

Consider the strategy of using dramatic instruction to convey critical content. In this strategy, the teacher asks students to participate in a dramatic activity that reinforces the critical content. Dramatic activities can range from skits and role playing to hand gestures and other body movements. For example, a group of elementary students might act out an investigation to find a missing animal using mathematics clues.

Highlighting critical information helps students attend to the most important content out of all the content they encounter each day. Figure 6.4 depicts the self-reflection scale for highlighting critical information.

Score	Description
4: Innovating	I adapt behaviors and create new strategies for unique student needs and situations.
3: Applying	I signal to students which content is critical versus noncritical, and I monitor the extent to which students are attending to critical information.
2: Developing	I signal to students which content is critical versus noncritical, but I do not monitor the effect on students.
1: Beginning	I use the strategies and behaviors associated with this element incorrectly or with parts missing.
0: Not Using	I am unaware of strategies and behaviors associated with this element.

Figure 6.4: Self-rating scale for element 16—Highlighting critical information.

Element 17: Reviewing Content

Reviewing content means helping or prompting students to revisit content they have already learned. Teachers often use this element when students have read a text that includes several concepts, and the goal is to summarize what they have read. It can also be useful in the mathematics classroom. The focus of reviewing content strategies should not be on reviewing all the algorithms and steps associated with an operation but instead on reviewing multiple ways to reason through mathematics problems.

The reason-talk-choose protocol we show in figure 6.5, asks students to review multiple strategies first individually and then in a group before deciding if they would solve a problem the same way or differently the next time they encounter it based on new reasoning. This protocol is a tool for the strategy of presenting a problem, demonstrating questioning, and summary.

Reason

1. Give students a problem and ask them to independently write out how they would solve the problem to share their reasoning.
2. Instruct students to get into groups and share their reasoning with other group members.
3. Each group member then summarizes another student's reasoning.
4. A scribe from the group records the different approaches on chart paper or in an online talk.

Talk

5. Give a prompt: "Which solution path took the fewest steps?" or "Which path made you think, Aha! I've never thought of it that way before!"
6. The small groups respond to the prompts in group discussion.

Choose

7. Students choose a strategy shared during group work or a new strategy they would like to use the next time they solve a similar problem, explaining why they would choose that strategy, their reasoning, and their solution path.

Figure 6.5: Reason-talk-choose protocol.

*Visit **go.SolutionTree.com/instruction** for a free reproducible version of this figure.*

This protocol empowers students to deepen their understanding of concepts and build critical thinking skills by choosing the strategy that makes the most sense to them. When prompting students to use this protocol, it's effective to pose numerical problems that either have one answer with multiple pathways to that answer or that have more than one possible answer. Problems with multiple answers increase the chance of a variety of reasoning paths.

Another effective strategy for reviewing content is the use of cloze activities, specifically cloze passages. Cloze passages help to build student familiarity with text structures, vocabulary, and comprehension.

With this strategy, teachers first rewrite a mathematics passage placing a blank line in place of strategic words. Have students read the passage and try to determine from context the words that might fit in the blanks. Read the correct passage to the whole class and allow students to reflect on their work. Discuss whether words students chose that differ from the author's make sense in the context of the passage.

- **Student team summary:** Have groups write or draw what they learned the previous day and share with the class. For this activity, students who are listening to the summary should ask the group questions and provide feedback, like in a Socratic discussion. The feedback to students is immediate, and the teacher can document group understanding to use in planning for the next day.
- **Questioning:** Use this strategy in small groups or whole groups. Ask students questions such as—
  - "Why?"
  - "Could you explain it another way?"
  - "How does this connect with . . . ?"

  Questions must be crafted to facilitate a conversation that provides feedback on student understanding. Through the questioning process, students receive immediate feedback, which helps them shape their understanding in the moment. As a teacher, you are responding formatively by listening and choosing your next question based on student answers. This formative assessment makes it an effective previewing strategy.

Reviewing content provides students with the opportunity to recall material that they have learned. Figure 6.6 depicts the self-reflection scale for reviewing content.

Score	Description
4: Innovating	I adapt behaviors and create new strategies for unique student needs and situations.
3: Applying	I engage students in a brief review of content that highlights the critical information, and I monitor the extent to which students can recall and describe previous content.
2: Developing	I engage students in a brief review of content that highlights the critical information, but I do not monitor the effect on students.
1: Beginning	I use the strategies and behaviors associated with this element incorrectly or with parts missing.
0: Not Using	I am unaware of strategies and behaviors associated with this element.

Figure 6.6: Self-rating scale for element 17—Reviewing content.

Element 18: Revising Knowledge

The difference between reviewing and revising knowledge is that revising knowledge involves changing, adding to, or deleting what students have previously learned.

A Frayer Model (figure 6.7) is a great tool to use in the mathematics classroom to help students revise knowledge. Have students write the word they are going to define in the middle of the graphic organizer. In the upper left corner, have students write the definition in their own words. In the upper right corner, have students write the facts or characteristics they know about the word. In the lower left corner, have students write or draw an example of the word. In the lower right corner, have students write or draw a nonexample of the word.

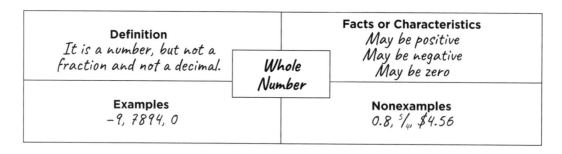

Figure 6.7: Frayer Model for revising knowledge.

Figure 6.8 depicts the self-rating scale for element 18, revising knowledge.

Score	Description
4: Innovating	I adapt behaviors and create new strategies for unique student needs and situations.
3: Applying	I engage students in revision of previous content, and I monitor the extent to which these revisions deepen students' understanding.
2: Developing	I engage students in revision of previous content, but I do not monitor the effect on students.
1: Beginning	I use the strategies and behaviors associated with this element incorrectly or with parts missing.
0: Not Using	I am unaware of strategies and behaviors associated with this element.

Figure 6.8: Self-rating scale for element 18—Revising knowledge.

Element 19: Reflecting on Learning

Strategies for reflecting on learning not only focus students' attention on the content but also on themselves as learners. In the mathematics classroom, when students reflect on their learning, they understand how and why their thinking about mathematics has changed while developing their reasoning and communication skills. Additionally, students build critical-thinking ability by recognizing cause-and-effect relationships. Several strategies for prompting student reflection include reflection journals, think logs, exit slips, and knowledge comparisons.

An effective activity to support reflective thinking in the mathematics classroom using the strategy of knowledge comparisons is the "I used to think, and now I think" activity adapted from Richard F. Elmore (2011). This strategy is useful whenever students' initial thoughts based on prior learning have changed as a result of new learning. Students write a reflection prompted by the statement, "I used to think, and now I think. . . ." An example of this reflection routine for middle school appears in figure 6.9. Elementary students could write about fractions or place value. High school students could reflect about linear equations or derivatives. Teachers can use this activity with students while using the reflection journal strategy, think logs, and as an exit slip activity.

I used to think, and now I think. . . .

When we began this study of multiplying decimals, I had some idea what it was all about. I used to think it was just about following the rules of multiplication. You know, first multiply as if there is no decimal, and then count the number of digits after the decimal in each factor. Then I put the same number of digits behind the decimal in the product. I have been thinking about how my ideas about multiplication have changed as a result of what I've been working on for my passion project. Now I think about how I use math to help me figure out things that I care about. For my project, I'm starting a YouTube channel, and I want to find out how many viewers it would take to make a certain amount of money. I multiplied number of viewers I hope to gain by the percentage of revenue for every ad viewed. I think about math differently now, as a way of helping me make money or learn about investments.

Figure 6.9: I used to think, and now I think. . . . reflection.

Figure 6.10 depicts the self-reflection scale for element 19, reflecting on learning.

Score	Description
4: Innovating	I adapt behaviors and create new strategies for unique student needs and situations.
3: Applying	I engage students in reflecting on their own learning and the learning process, and I monitor the extent to which students self-assess their understanding and effort.
2: Developing	I engage students in reflecting on their own learning and the learning process, but I do not monitor the effect on students.
1: Beginning	I use the strategies and behaviors associated with this element incorrectly or with parts missing.
0: Not Using	I am unaware of strategies and behaviors associated with this element.

Figure 6.10: Self-rating scale for element 19—Reflecting on learning.

Element 20: Assigning Purposeful Homework

Many teachers assign homework as a matter of routine rather than as purposeful practice. As research suggests, homework is perhaps one of the most misused strategies in K–12 classrooms (see Marzano & Pickering, 2007a, 2007b, 2007c). Mathematics teachers must assign homework purposefully, using it only when needed.

Mathematics teachers frequently use homework, but not always in ways that enhance student learning. Purposeful homework should include formative independent practice. Additionally, when assigning homework, teachers should consider to what degree the homework task promotes problem solving and reasoning. Figure 6.11 can help with assessing the cognitive demand of independent mathematics practice activities.

Lower-Level Cognitive Demand	Higher-Level Cognitive Demand
Memorization: Requires eliciting information, such as a fact, definition, term, or a simple procedure, as well as performing a simple algorithm or applying a formula	**Procedures with connections:** Requires complex reasoning, planning, using evidence, and explanations of thinking
Procedures without connections: Requires the engagement of some mental processing beyond a recall of information	**Doing mathematics:** Requires complex reasoning, planning, developing, and thinking most likely over an extended period of time

Source: Adapted from Smith & Stein, 2012.

Figure 6.11: Tool for assessing cognitive demand.

When assigning mathematics homework, keep the following important questions in mind.

1. Is there an alignment to the current learning standards (by unit)?
2. Is it appropriately balanced for cognitive demand?
3. Is it relevant and intrinsically motivating?
4. Is it appropriate in duration?
5. Does it meet your student's needs?

Figure 6.12 (page 64) represents the self-reflection scale for this element.

Score	Description
4: Innovating	I adapt behaviors and create new strategies for unique student needs and situations.
3: Applying	When appropriate (as opposed to routinely), I assign homework that is designed to deepen knowledge of information or provide practice with a skill, strategy, or process, and I monitor the extent to which students understand the homework.
2: Developing	When appropriate (as opposed to routinely), I assign homework that is designed to deepen knowledge of information or provide practice with a skill, strategy, or process, but I do not monitor the effect on students.
1: Beginning	I use the strategies and behaviors associated with this element incorrectly or with parts missing.
0: Not Using	I am unaware of strategies and behaviors associated with this element.

Figure 6.12: Self-rating scale for element 20—Assigning purposeful homework.

Element 21: Elaborating on Information

Elaboration is the process of going beyond what one has initially learned. In mathematics, elaboration supports students in going below the surface of basic mathematical concepts. *The New Art and Science of Teaching* framework focuses on questioning strategies for this element.

Using Questioning

Keilani Stolk's (2013) study evaluated categories of questions that are part of conceptual mathematics-based classrooms. These are classrooms in which students investigate or explain beyond what they already know to create a new understanding of processes, justifications, or modifications or existing processes or justifications. This pressing of students to think beyond what they have previously done or thought pushes them to progress to a higher level of mathematical thought or understanding.

The four categories are (1) exploring to construct a justification, (2) exploring to construct a process, (3) exploring to modify a process, and (4) exploring to modify a justification. Figure 6.13, adapted from Stolk (2013), provides descriptions of each of these categories and examples of questions that can engage students in complex ways of thinking about mathematics in each category. Teachers can use these prompts in small-group discourse or during whole-group discussions.

Category	Description	Examples
Exploring to construct a justification	Engaging students in creating or understanding a justification for or explanation of a mathematical concept	"How can we reconcile the idea that [this] has to be equal to [that]?" "Why does that get you the right answer?'
Exploring to construct a process	Engaging students in constructing or understanding a mathematical process	"How can you determine if you're right?" "Can you think of a different way to do this problem?" "How can you solve this?"
Exploring to modify a process	Engaging students in modifying an existing process so it can be used in a different mathematical situation	"Would this work with [other numbers]?" "What about in this example? Try doing the same thing."
Exploring to modify a justification	Engaging students in modifying an existing justification to explain or justify a different mathematical situation	"Will that always give me something that works?" "How can you explain that [this] is always equal to [that]?"

Source: Adapted from Stolk, 2013.

Figure 6.13: Questions for engaging students in complex ways of thinking in four categories.

As figure 6.13 shows, teachers can help students elaborate on their thinking by engaging them in using specific types of questions. A question geared for justification may not be the best question to help construct a process.

Expressing Dilemmas

Another activity to support students in elaborating on information in the mathematics classroom is allowing them to describe dilemmas, challenges they are experiencing while solving real-world mathematics problems—something that is problematic or has not been as effective as they would like it to be that is related to a project, unit question, essential question, or mathematics scenario. This activity uses the probing questions and focus questions strategies from *The New Art and Science of Teaching* framework. This helps students think more expansively about a mathematics concept or a dilemma they are facing and enables them to find the support and mindset to push through challenges. We adapted the Expressing Dilemma Protocol from the Consultancy Protocol (Dunne, Evans, & Thompson-Grove, 2017) to help teachers solve dilemmas in the profession. The eight steps of the adapted protocol help students solve dilemmas in mathematics, deepening and enhancing their understanding of content and material as well as supporting critical thinking and elaboration.

1. The teacher begins by organizing students into small groups of four to seven students. One student is a presenter while the others are the consultancy group, which gives students feedback.
2. The presenter gives an overview of the dilemma with which he or she is struggling, and frames a question for the consultancy group to consider. The focus of the group's conversation is on the dilemma the student presenter explains. The consultancy group asks *clarifying questions*—that is, questions that have brief, factual answers. For example, "How many nickels does she have left?" "How long it take you to solve the problem?" and "Did you get a remainder?" (This step should take about five minutes.)

3. The group members then ask probing questions of the presenter. They should word these questions so that they help the presenter clarify and expand her or his thinking about the dilemma. For example, "How did you determine how many nickels she had left?", "Why did you draw number bonds when you solved the problem?", and "What does the remainder mean in this solution?" The goal is for the presenter to learn more about the question she or he framed and to do some analysis. The presenter responds to the group's questions, although sometimes a probing question might ask the presenter to see the dilemma in a novel way that the presenter might not have an immediate response to beyond, "I never thought to approach the problem this way." There is no discussion by the student group of the presenter's responses. At the end of ten minutes, the group leader or teacher asks the presenter to restate her or his probing question for the group.

4. The teacher frames a focus question for the student consultancy group. The question is around the dilemma that seems to be the crux of the problem. The focus question will guide the student group in its discussion of the dilemma. Figure 6.14 provides three detailed examples of framed focus questions. All students then critique the focus question. Questions they may ask include, "Is this question important to my dilemma? Is this question important to my learning? Is this question important to others in my group?"

Elementary example: You are part of the design team for an amusement park. The residents of your town want a rollercoaster, a Ferris wheel, and a water slide. The 0.5- by 0.5-mile area will allow for only two of these rides. How will you use this area to make the residents of the town happy?

Intermediate example: You are the CEO for a tech start-up that has developed an app to help tutor students in mathematics. The initial investment was $50,000. The software will cost $20,000 in engineering costs plus the amount of labor costs for software developers. How much more money will you need to operate the business in the first year? When will you be able to pay your investors? What will your cash flow be like? How much will you sell the app for?

Secondary example: The school wants to install a green roof. The roof is circular and some room must be left for maintenance. What's the best way to create the maximum space for greenery and allow a small space for maintenance? Give dimensions and the shape of the space the greenery will occupy.

Figure 6.14: Framed focus questions.

5. After sharing the dilemma with the small group, the presenter ends the description by asking a specific and thoughtful question, "What do you *really* want to know? What is your real dilemma?" The dilemma is the problem group members face when tackling the question. There are some things that are known, so that information shouldn't be in the question (such as information specifically given in the scenario). This question will help the student group focus its feedback. Yes-or-no questions generally provide less feedback, so they should be avoided. With this step, presenters have the opportunity to tap into the thoughts of the group.

6. The group members then talk with each other about the dilemma. In this step, the group works to define the issues more thoroughly and objectively. Sometimes members of the group suggest actions the presenter might consider taking; if they do, they should frame them as suggestions made only after the group has thoroughly analyzed the dilemma. The presenter doesn't speak during this discussion, but listens and takes notes. This step should take about fifteen minutes.

Possible questions to spark conversation within the discussion include:

- What did we hear?
- What didn't we hear that might be relevant?

- What assumptions seem to be operating?
- What questions does the dilemma raise for us?
- What do we think about the dilemma?
- What might we do or try if faced with a similar dilemma?
- What have we done in similar situations?

7. The student presenter then reflects on what she or he heard and on what he or she is now thinking, sharing with the group anything that particularly resonated for him or her during any part of the group work. This step should take about five minutes.

8. The teacher then leads a brief conversation about the group's observation of the consultancy process. This step should take about five minutes.

Elaboration is an inferential act that fosters new awareness when students engage in it effectively. Figure 6.15 depicts the self-reflection scale for this element.

Score	Description
4: Innovating	I adapt behaviors and create new strategies for unique student needs and situations.
3: Applying	I ask students to elaborate on information, and I monitor the extent to which my actions affect students' responses.
2: Developing	I ask students to elaborate on information, but I do not monitor the effect on students.
1: Beginning	I use the strategies and behaviors associated with this element incorrectly or with parts missing.
0: Not Using	I am unaware of strategies and behaviors associated with this element.

Figure 6.15: Self-rating scale for element 21—Elaborating on information.

Element 22: Organizing Students to Interact

Organizing students in ways that allow them to explain and justify their thinking not only deepens conceptual knowledge and complexity in thought but also supports the development of social learning skills, such as skills in communicating, collaborating, and expressing creativity. *The New Art and Science of Teaching* framework describes the strategies of grouping students for active processing, cooperative learning, and peer-response groups for this element. Following are some prompts mathematics teachers can use to organize students to interact in these meaningful ways using the activities that follow the list (world café, chalk talk, the Charrette protocol, and why-what-how).

- **Elementary:** Give students an assortment of twenty shapes, which include quadrilaterals, nonquadrilaterals, regular polygons, and not-regular polygons. Ask students to organize the shapes into the four different categories on a grid. This activity specifically prompts students to look at shapes that fall into the quadrilateral, polygon section of the grid. From this, students will have an opportunity to make observations about the shapes, identifying parallel lines, ninety-degree angles, equal sides, and so on. Once students have sorted the shapes, they record the different qualities or attributes of each quadrilateral on poster paper. The collaborative structures in the list that follows (world café, chalk talk, Charrette protocol, and why-what-how) help frame discussions around what to do with the poster papers. The end goal is to discover attributes of the shapes students have sorted.

- **Intermediate:** Provide students with the following prompt—At a local movie theater, you can buy two large sodas and a box of popcorn for $11.00. If you only want one large soda and a box of popcorn, it will cost $8.00. How much does the box of popcorn cost? Students use the collaborative structures in the list that follows (world café, chalk talk, Charrette protocol, and why-what-how) to solve the problem.
- **Secondary:** Ask students how they could categorize graphs of polynomial functions based on end behavior. Once students determine in groups how they could categorize the graphs (with the equation written on graph paper), create a space on a wall for each category and have students tape their graphs up on the wall. Have students work in the collaborative structures you choose from the list that follows (world café, chalk talk, Charrette protocol, and why-what-how) to discuss the patterns and observations they made.

World Café

In a world café, students sit with their group at a table with a "tablecloth" (paper) on which students record their thoughts about a question. Students can discuss problems or topics with their group, and then rotate so they are exposed to the notes of other teams. This protocol also encourages students to rotate leadership roles and provides diversity in grouping.

Chalk Talk

This strategy prompts students to use silent response as a tool to help them explore a topic or mathematics problem in depth. On a large piece of paper, whiteboard, or tablet, students respond to the problem, writing the steps they are taking, operations they are using, data they are referring to, and so on. Other students make notes in different colors, responding to other students' thinking, reasoning, and viewpoints. This is an effective strategy for getting those students involved who are not as likely to participate in a verbal discussion, and it helps students develop better observation and listening skills.

Charrette Protocol

The Charrette protocol is useful when students are struggling through a problem and are stuck—when they aren't sure how to move forward. Students bring their struggle to the group, focusing on a question such as, "How should I proceed?" Students are not asking for the answer. Rather, they are seeking advice, guidance, and strategies from their group members that they might not have thought about yet.

Why-What-How

In this activity, students work cooperatively in small groups to engage in mathematics discourse. They ask:

- "Why was this a problem worth solving?"
- "What solution am I trying to find? What problem am I solving?"
- "How did I solve the problem?"

Each student shares his or her why-what-how.

These collaborative opportunities have one thing in common. They all focus not on the correct answer or one right solution path but rather on all the possible methods of finding the answer.

Figure 6.16 depicts the self-reflection scale for element 22, organizing students to interact.

Score	Description
4: Innovating	I adapt behaviors and create new strategies for unique student needs and situations.
3: Applying	I organize students to interact in a thoughtful way that facilitates collaboration, and I monitor the extent to which students collaborate.
2: Developing	I organize students to interact in a thoughtful way that facilitates collaboration, but I do not monitor the effect on students.
1: Beginning	I use the strategies and behaviors associated with this element incorrectly or with parts missing.
0: Not Using	I am unaware of strategies and behaviors associated with this element.

Figure 6.16: Self-rating scale for element 22—Organizing students to interact.

GUIDING QUESTIONS FOR CURRICULUM DESIGN

For using strategies that appear in all types of lessons—direct instruction, practicing and deepening, and knowledge application lessons—this is the design question: *Throughout all types of lessons, what strategies will I use to help students continually integrate new knowledge with old knowledge and revise their understanding accordingly?* The following specific questions align to each of the eight elements in this chapter and serve to guide teachers in planning instruction. Although theoretically teachers could incorporate all elements in every kind of lesson, this would not necessarily be wise practice. Rather, teachers should use their professional judgment to judiciously balance the use of these elements.

- **Element 15:** How will I help students preview content?

_____

_____

_____

_____

- **Element 16:** How will I highlight critical information?

_____

_____

_____

_____

- **Element 17:** How will I help students review content?

_____

_____

_____

_____

- **Element 18:** How will I help students revise knowledge?

_____

_____

_____

_____

- **Element 19:** How will I help students reflect on their learning?

_____

_____

_____

_____

- **Element 20:** How will I use purposeful homework?

_____

_____

_____

_____

- **Element 21:** How will I help students elaborate on information?

_____

_____

_____

_____

- **Element 22:** How will I organize students to interact?

_____

_____

_____

_____

Summary

Using strategies that appear in all types of lessons involves eight elements: (1) previewing strategies, (2) highlighting critical information, (3) reviewing content, (4) revising knowledge, (5) reflecting on learning, (6) assigning purposeful homework, (7) elaborating on information, and (8) organizing students to interact. In the mathematics classroom, these elements operationalize in a variety of ways. Using the strategies discussed in this chapter, mathematics teachers ensure students are actively engaged in each part of the lesson and learning experience. They will plan for the type of student discourse that best connects to the outcomes of the lesson and that best connects to student interests and learning styles. The strategies addressed in this chapter ensure that students are developing mathematical thinking such as reasoning, problem solving, and justification skills.

PART III
Context

CHAPTER 7

Using Engagement Strategies

The broad category of context refers to students' mental readiness during the teaching-learning process. Specifically, for students to be ready to learn, their needs must be met relative to engagement, order, a sense of belonging, and a sense of high expectations. Engagement, the focus of the seventh design area, is the gateway to such readiness.

Engagement can mean a wide variety of things in the mathematics classroom. It can be the simple act of students knowing what the teacher is doing. It can also refer to students' being intrinsically motivated by what occurs in class. In *The New Art and Science of Teaching* framework, engagement involves four mental states, each one somewhat dependent on the state immediately preceding it.

The first mental state is attention—students attending to what is occurring in the classroom. Some of the strategies in this chapter focus on accomplishing this rather straightforward but important aspect of engagement. A second mental state is sufficient levels of energy. The elements and strategies in this mental state are designed to increase students' energy levels when they are getting low. A third mental state is intrigue. The elements and strategies that address intrigue in this chapter help stimulate high levels of student interest so that students seek further information about the content on their own. The fourth mental state is inspiration. As the name implies, the elements and strategies that focus on this state spark students' desire for self-agency and propel them to engage in tasks of their own design and control.

There are ten elements focused on engagement in *The New Art and Science of Teaching* framework: noticing and reacting when students are not engaged (element 23), increasing response rates (element 24), using physical movement (element 25), maintaining a lively pace (element 26), demonstrating intensity and enthusiasm (element 27), presenting unusual information (element 28), using friendly controversy (element 29), using academic games (element 30), providing opportunities for students to talk about themselves (element 31), and motivating and inspiring students (element 32).

In this chapter we address six of these ten elements: noticing and reacting when students are not engaged (element 23), using physical movement (element 25), presenting unusual information (element 28), using friendly controversy (element 29), using academic games (element 30), and providing opportunities for students to talk about themselves (element 31).

Element 23: Noticing and Reacting When Students Are Not Engaged

Teachers must be aware when students are not engaged and be prepared to react by implementing appropriate strategies to re-engage students. Executing this element can take many forms in the mathematics classroom. *The New Art and Science of Teaching* framework identifies monitoring individual student engagement, monitoring overall class engagement, and using self-reported student engagement data as strategies for this element. The framework also identifies the need to re-engage individual students. The tool in figure 7.1 allows students to vent any frustrations they are having through an open feedback system. It is helpful for analyzing frustrations and re-engaging students after the teacher has given feedback.

Cycle Phase	Student Feedback	Teacher Feedback
Purpose (Why)		
Problem (What)		
Proactive Planning (How)		
Comments:		

Figure 7.1: Open feedback system tool.

*Visit **go.SolutionTree.com/instruction** for a free reproducible version of this figure.*

To use the tool in figure 7.1, invite students to give feedback not only on their own progress but also on how they feel you have supported their learning and growth. The fact that this cycle is truly two-way allows students to develop stronger trust in the teacher and more effectively synthesize feedback (due to a more positive environment of open communication).

Every conversation in the feedback protocol begins with identifying the *why*, or *purpose* of a task. This must take place before addressing any problem—or *what*—as the problem will lack context if the purpose isn't clear. The problem is the challenge a student is facing with the concept or a task that the student and the teacher will explore. Finally, proactive planning is the *how* of the cycle, where the teacher and the student decide on steps they should take to solve the problem (re-engaging the student) to accomplish the goals identified in the purpose. The comment box in figure 7.1 provides a space for the teacher and student to continue the dialogue or record reflections on the feedback they receive. The teacher and student can most effectively leverage this tool digitally through a collaborative cloud-based document.

Figure 7.2 depicts the self-reflection scale for this element about noticing and reacting when students are disengaged.

Score	Description
4: Innovating	I adapt behaviors and create new strategies for unique student needs and situations.
3: Applying	I notice and react when students are not engaged, and I monitor the extent to which my actions affect students' engagement.
2: Developing	I notice and react when students are not engaged, but I do not monitor the effect on students.
1: Beginning	I use the strategies and behaviors associated with this element incorrectly or with parts missing.
0: Not Using	I am unaware of strategies and behaviors associated with this element.

Figure 7.2: Self-rating scale for element 23—Noticing and reacting when students are not engaged.

Element 25: Using Physical Movement

Physical movement has a direct connection to students' energy levels. As Marzano (2017) states, this makes sense since movement is related to increased energy. It also makes sense physiologically: movement increases blood flow to the brain, stimulating engagement (Marzano & Pickering, 2011). Learning mathematics is more effective and easier when teachers combine it with movement. Faculty at the University of Copenhagen (2017) find that when students use movement while learning, they improve at mathematics, regardless of whether the impact of the activity is high or low. After the six-week study, students who learned while doing whole-body movement saw their mathematics skills increase by nearly 8 percent. They had about four more correct responses than the baseline, and twice as much improvement as the sedentary group.

Incorporating movement into mathematics lessons doesn't need to be complicated. At the elementary level, teachers can incorporate movement using mathematics-themed songs and dances, playing math games like math hopscotch or a math scavenger hunt, and asking students to recall math facts while walking to lunch or recess. Young students in grades K–2 can make shapes or numerals using their bodies. Older elementary and secondary students can play games like a math race where they compete in challenges involving mathematics and mathematics Pictionary with math concepts or vocabulary. Students of all ages can write and perform songs or rap music with math themes and perform for the class or school. Students can move around the classroom to various mathematics stations that ask them to solve problems in different areas of the classroom.

Energy is essential to engagement; physical movement is a straightforward approach to raising energy. Figure 7.3 depicts the self-reflection scale for this element about incorporating physical movement into the classroom.

Score	Description
4: Innovating	I adapt behaviors and create new strategies for unique student needs and situations.
3: Applying	I use physical movement to maintain student engagement, and I monitor the extent to which these activities enhance student engagement.
2: Developing	I use physical movement to maintain student engagement, but I do not monitor the effect on students.
1: Beginning	I use the strategies and behaviors associated with this element incorrectly or with parts missing.
0: Not Using	I am unaware of strategies and behaviors associated with this element.

Figure 7.3: Self-rating scale for element 25—Using physical movement.

Element 28: Presenting Unusual Information

One of the primary responsibilities of teachers is to make the content they teach interesting to students. We know students will engage authentically in content when they're intrigued and interested by it. In mathematics, teachers often struggle to frame the subject as inherently exciting. Traditional mathematics instruction has focused on equations or operations, which admittedly do not interest most people. Rather, excitement for mathematics often happens when students get unexpected results.

Presenting unusual and counterintuitive information is a strategy *The New Art and Science of Teaching* framework identifies to aid in engagement in mathematics. In a debate with journalist Malcolm Gladwell, psychologist Adam Grant (2018) states that ideas catch fire not because they're true, but because they're interesting. What makes ideas interesting? An idea is interesting when it departs from conventional wisdom or is different than what one expected. In the area of mathematics, however, teachers aren't challenging deeply rooted assumptions; they are sharing information that might be counter to how students view that concept. For example, in today's classrooms, teachers are asking students to decompose numbers. Traditionally, students have been asked to add numbers. This changed because researchers and educators now understand that students learn mathematics better when they are able to see the groupings, relationships, and patterns in numbers.

Teachers can use the following intrigue-explain-wonder protocol to help students discuss unusual information in the mathematics classroom. Teachers first expose students to a scenario that relates to mathematics. Then students address the following three questions.

1. Why is this intriguing?
2. How do you explain it?
3. What does it make you wonder about now?

Figure 7.4 includes examples of unusual and extraordinary mathematics scenarios. Scenarios 1, 2, and 3 are appropriate for middle and high school, and scenario 4 is appropriate for the elementary level. Scenario 4 is a perfect prelude to a STEM activity, where students could make slime, which requires altering ingredients and quantities, measuring ratios, and performing unit conversions.

Scenario 1:
The birthday paradox is a probability concept. It states that if there are 23 people in a room, there is a more than 50 percent chance that two people will have the same birthday. It seems counterintuitive because the probability of having a birthday on any particular day is only 1/365.
Scenario 2:
If you shuffle a pack of cards properly, chances are that exact order has never been seen before in the whole history of the universe.
Scenario 3:
Suppose you're on a game show, and you're given the choice of three doors. Behind one door is a car; behind the others, goats. You pick a door, say number one. The host, who knows what's behind the doors, opens another door, say number three, which has a goat. He then says to you, "Do you want to pick door number two?" Is it to your advantage to switch your choice? Surprisingly, the answer is that it's better to switch!
Scenario 4:
Slime is made of polymers, which is kind of like spaghetti. How is this possible?

Intrigue-Explain-Wonder Protocol

- Why is this *intriguing*?

- How do you *explain* it?

- What does it make you *wonder* about now?

Figure 7.4: Intrigue-explain-wonder scenarios and protocol.

*Visit **go.SolutionTree.com/instruction** for a free reproducible version of this figure.*

It's important that teachers expose students to fun, interesting, and unusual mathematical paradoxes and problems to stimulate their interest and intrigue, and also to provide the opportunity for students to engage in conjecture about possible solutions and discuss why a scenario might be particularly baffling to them.

Figure 7.5 depicts the self-reflection scale for element 28, presenting unusual information.

Score	Description
4: Innovating	I adapt behaviors and create new strategies for unique student needs and situations.
3: Applying	I use unusual or intriguing information to capture students' attention, and I monitor the extent to which this information enhances engagement.
2: Developing	I use unusual or intriguing information to capture students' attention, but I do not monitor the effect on students.
1: Beginning	I use the strategies and behaviors associated with this element incorrectly or with parts missing.
0: Not Using	I am unaware of strategies and behaviors associated with this element.

Figure 7.5: Self-rating scale for element 28—Presenting unusual information.

Element 29: Using Friendly Controversy

Strategies within this element stimulate students to be intrigued and interested. This is a natural by-product of controversy. When students disagree with someone, they are usually highly engaged. Francesca Gino (2018), a professor at Harvard Business School, conducted several studies concluding that nonconforming behaviors support student confidence, innovation, and performance.

One study recruited employees from different companies and asked group members to behave in nonconforming ways at work over a series of weeks, such as voicing alternative opinions from their colleagues, expressing their true ideas or feelings rather than those they were expected to have, or proposing ideas that their colleagues might find unorthodox. Gino asked another group to behave in conforming ways for three weeks, such as staying quiet and nodding along even when they disagreed with a colleague's decision. Lastly, she asked the control group to behave as usual during this time. After three weeks had passed, members of the first group indicated that they felt more confident and engaged in their jobs than members of the other two groups. They were also more creative when completing a task they were given as part of a three-week follow-up survey, and their supervisors rated them higher on both innovation and performance.

In another experiment, Adam Grant (2016) sought to show how nonconformity promotes a culture of originality. He found a pilot in the U.S. Navy, Ben Kohlmann, who was known for being a troublemaker, dissenter, disrupter, heretic, and radical. He searched for others within the Navy who were also known to be nonconformists and insubordinate. He started with this small group and then began expanding his network. He recruited members who had never shown a desire to challenge the status quo and exposed them to new ways of thinking. They visited centers of innovation excellence outside the military, from Google to the Rocky Mountain Institute. They engaged in readings on innovation and created opportunities to engage in regular debates about ideas. Soon they pioneered the use of 3-D printers on ships and a robotic fish for stealth underwater missions, and other rapid-innovation cells began springing up around the military. What can we learn about nonconformity and friendly controversy from this study? When learners discover their voice, they gain confidence and momentum to learn and spread ideas.

One way students can get engaged through the strategy of friendly controversy is by exercising their voice during debates (as opposed to solving another mathematics problem about trains leaving stations or what percentage of a cake each student gets). Teachers can spark debate by prompting students with scenarios. Figure 7.6 shows some examples of prompts to help spark debates.

Elementary scenario:

Albert and Bernard have just become friends with Cheryl, and they want to know when her birthday is. Cheryl gives them a list of ten possible dates.

Month	Date					
May		15	16			19
June				17	18	
July	14		16			
August	14	15		17		

Cheryl then tells Albert and Bernard separately the month (Albert) and the day (Bernard) of her birthday.

Albert: I don't know when Cheryl's birthday is, but I know that Bernard doesn't know either.

Bernard: At first I didn't know when Cheryl's birthday is, but I know now.

Albert: Then I also know when Cheryl's birthday is.

So when is Cheryl's birthday?

Justify your answer and explain how you arrived there.

Answer:

To solve this problem, we need to look carefully at the question and then work through each statement to see what we can deduce from it.

- From the question, we know that Cheryl told Albert May, June, July, or August.
- Cheryl told Bernard 14, 15, 16, 17, 18, or 19.

Albert: "I don't know when Cheryl's birthday is, but I know that Bernard does not know either."

- Cheryl told Bernard the day of her birthday. There are only two days, 18 and 19, that appear once on Cheryl's list. This means that Cheryl's birthday cannot be May 19 or June 18. If it was, then Bernard would know the answer.

- Remember that Cheryl told Albert the month, and from the statement, we can deduce that he knows that Bernard does not know the birthday. For Albert to be certain that Bernard does not know Cheryl's birthday, the month Cheryl told Albert must not have been May or June.

- Therefore, Cheryl's birthday must be in July or August.

Bernard: "At first I didn't know when Cheryl's birthday is, but I know now."

- Bernard has worked out that Cheryl's birthday is in July or August.

- If Bernard now knows Cheryl's birthday, the day Cheryl told him would be the 15th, 16th, or 17th. It cannot be the 14th as this date is a possibility for both July and August, and, as such, Bernard wouldn't know Cheryl's birthday for certain.

Albert: "Then I also know when Cheryl's birthday is."

- Albert has worked out that Cheryl's birthday is one of the following:

  - July 16

  - August 15

  - August 17

- If Albert now knows for certain when Cheryl's birthday is, she must have told him the month of July. If it had been August, there would be two possible options.

Therefore, the answer is July 16.

Intermediate scenario:

The Paradox of Achilles and the Tortoise is one of a number of theoretical discussions of movement put forward by the Greek philosopher Zeno of Elea in the 5th century BC. It begins with the great hero Achilles challenging a tortoise to a footrace. To keep things fair, he agrees to give the tortoise a head start of, say, 500 meters. When the race begins, Achilles unsurprisingly starts running at a speed much faster than the tortoise, so that by the time he has reached the 500 meter mark, the tortoise has only walked 50 meters further than him. But by the time Achilles has reached the 550 meter mark, the tortoise has walked another 5 meters. And by the time he has reached the 555 meter mark, the tortoise has walked another 0.5 meters, then 0.25 meters, then 0.125 meters, and so on. This process continues again and again over an infinite series of smaller and smaller distances, with the tortoise always moving forward while Achilles always plays catch up.

How is it possible that Achilles overtakes the tortoise?

Answer:

Suppose we take Zeno's Paradox at face value for the moment, and agree with him that before I can walk a mile, I must first walk a half mile. And before I can walk the remaining half mile, I must first cover half of it; that is, I must walk a quarter of a mile, and then an eighth of a mile, and then a sixteenth of a mile, and then a thirty-second of a mile, and so on. Well, suppose I could cover all these infinite number of small distances: how far should I have walked? One mile! In other words:

$$1 = \tfrac{1}{2} + \tfrac{1}{4} + \tfrac{1}{8} + \tfrac{1}{16} + \tfrac{1}{32} \ldots$$

Figure 7.6: Mathematics scenarios to spark debate.

continued →

At first, this may seem impossible: adding up an infinite number of positive distances should give an infinite distance for the sum, but it doesn't. In this case, it gives a finite sum; indeed, all these distances add up to 1! A little reflection will reveal that this isn't so strange after all: if we can divide a finite distance into an infinite number of small distances, then adding all those distances together should produce the finite distance we started with. (An infinite sum is known in mathematics as an infinite series, and when such a sum adds up to a finite number, we say that the series is summable.)

Now, the resolution to Zeno's Paradox is easy. Think about it this way: Obviously, it will take fixed time to cross half the distance to the other side of a room, say two seconds. How long will it take to cross half of the remaining distance? Half as long—only one second. Covering half of the remaining distance (an eighth of the total) will take only half a second, and so on. So if I cross the room, covering all the infinitely many subdistances and adding up all the time it took to traverse them, it will have taken only four seconds.

Poor old Achilles would have won his race.

Secondary scenario:

The Banach-Tarski paradox is a theorem in a set theoretic geometry that states that a solid ball in three-dimensional space can be split into a finite number of nonoverlapping pieces, which can then be put back together in a different way to yield two identical copies of the original ball.

Explain how this is possible.

Answer:

Why is this a paradox? Well, it defies intuition because in our everyday lives, we normally never see one object magically turning into two equal copies of itself.

It's because it's not possible in our physical world. The mathematical version of the paradox uses the concept of an immeasurable set. Every object in real life is measurable, because it is the set of a finite number of atoms taking up a finite amount of space. Mathematically, even when finite becomes infinite, you still usually have measurable sets. You really have to try very hard in order to create an immeasurable set.

The Banach-Tarski paradox splits the sphere into a finite number of immeasurable sets of points. The key word is *finite*. In fact, it can be shown that it can be split into just FIVE pieces, one of them being the point at the center. So with the other four pieces, we can separate them into two groups of two, and create an entire sphere out of each group, each the same size as the original sphere.

Though this is impossible to do in real life (because we are bound by atoms), it is possible to make a real-life analogy. This analogy will require basic knowledge of the gas laws, namely, that pressure and volume are inversely related. Here we go:

Consider an easily stretchable balloon with some volume of gas inside it. Now release the gas into a container and divide the gas in the container to fill two balloons. Each new balloon will have one-half the volume of the original. But we're going to introduce a trick. We'll reduce the pressure of the room by half. This causes the balloons to each expand to double its size, so that each is as big as the original. We have reconstructed the paradox!

But wait, you say! Even though each new balloon has the same *volume* as the original, it has only one-half the density. So they're not the same balloon as the original.

That objection is correct for the physical world. But in mathematics, we CAN get two identical spheres out of one. Here's the catch: the mathematical sphere has infinite density. When you cut an infinite density in half, the new density is still infinity. This explains the paradox.

*Visit **go.SolutionTree.com/instruction** for a free reproducible version of this figure.*

Successful debate in the context of friendly controversy requires structure. Teachers should encourage students to share why they believe their series of steps is the best way to solve a mathematics problem; they must justify their thinking. Encourage students to actively and deeply listen to others' thinking and reasoning.

The argument-talk protocol in figure 7.7 (adapted from National School Reform Faculty [2015]) requires students to use critical-thinking skills to understand a presenter's assumptions and then share their own opinions related to the mathematics debate scenario.

To use the protocol, first put students into groups. Each student then presents his or her response to a mathematics problem or scenario. After each presenter shares, each group participant responds to the question prompts in figure 7.7. Continue the rounds for one prompt at a time. Then move to the next prompt.

Scenario: A beautiful penny-tiled floor was created using approximately 13,000 pennies. The homeowner provided this total number of pennies, but not the actual dimensions of the floor space he filled.

1. What **assumptions** does the presenter hold?
   The first presenter calculates the value to be $13,000. Other students think each value of a penny is $1.

2. What do you **agree** with in his or her argument?
   I agree that you need to use 13,000 as a multiplier.

3. What do you want to **disagree** with in his or her argument?
   I disagree that the value is $1, and believe the value is $0.01.

4. What parts of the argument do you **aspire to act on**?
   I'd like to show how I reach an answer of $130 for the solution.

Source: National School Reform Faculty, 2015.

Figure 7.7: Argument-talk protocol.

*Visit **go.SolutionTree.com/instruction** for a free reproducible version of this figure.*

Mathematics teachers can also use the strategies of class voting and opposite point of view that *The New Art and Science of Teaching* framework presents (Marzano, 2017). Using these strategies, students could vote on a particular solution to a mathematics problem, discussing the merits of each possibility, and then defend their point of view. When executed well, friendly controversy helps students analyze content with a critical eye. Figure 7.8 depicts the self-reflection scale for this element.

Score	Description
4: Innovating	I adapt behaviors and create new strategies for unique student needs and situations.
3: Applying	I use friendly controversy techniques to maintain student engagement, and I monitor the effect on students.
2: Developing	I use friendly controversy techniques to maintain student engagement, but I do not monitor the effect on students.
1: Beginning	I use the strategies and behaviors associated with this element incorrectly or with parts missing.
0: Not Using	I am unaware of strategies and behaviors associated with this element.

Figure 7.8: Self-rating scale for element 29—Using friendly controversy.

Element 30: Using Academic Games

Students who are reluctant to engage with mathematics will be much more willing to engage when they feel as if they are playing a game. *The New Art and Science of Teaching* framework suggests eight game strategies teachers can implement in the mathematics classroom (What Is the Question?, Name That Category, Talk a Mile a Minute, Classroom Feud, Which One Doesn't Belong?, using inconsequential competition, turning questions into games, and using vocabulary review games). In addition, we propose that mathematics teachers consider using a Rubik's Cube as a tool for academic games in the mathematics classroom. We believe it is one of the most effective mathematical game tools that a teacher can integrate into the classroom, from elementary to high school. Many students who struggle with motivation in mathematics are highly interested in solving the Rubik's Cube.

Mathematically, the Rubik's Cube is a *permutation group*—a group whose elements are permutations of a given set and whose group operation is the composition of these permutations. Teachers can explain this using algebra concepts for secondary students. Essentially, the cube represents six different colors and each color is repeated exactly nine times, so the cube can be considered an ordered list that has fifty-four elements with numbers between one and six, each number meaning a color being repeated nine times. Additionally, to play a Rubik's Cube, a person makes moves using any sequence of twists. A set of moves forms a group, where the group operation is a composition of moves. The group is large (43,252,003,274,489,856,000 elements), and includes many distinct subgroups (The Rubik's Cube, 2018). Because of the many combinations and approaches to playing the game, problem solving and perseverance are crucial parts of engaging with the Rubik's Cube. Additionally, there are many rigorous mathematics content connections that teachers can make with the game. Following are some ways to incorporate the Rubik's Cube at various levels of mathematics from the National Education Association (Nast, n.d.; www.nea.org/tools/lessons/71242.htm).

- **Shapes and polygons (elementary):** Students understand that attributes belonging to a category of two-dimensional figures also belong to all subcategories of that category. Students learn vocabulary about polygons using a vocabulary sheet and doing research online. They then apply what they have learned using a variety of questions.
- **Probability and statistics (intermediate):** Students explore the possible number of ways the pieces of a Rubik's Cube can be arranged.
- **How-to videos (secondary):** Students present information, findings, and supporting evidence using how-to videos so that other students can follow their line of reasoning. Students solidify their skills of solving a Rubik's Cube by teaching others.

The Rubik's Cube is an effective engagement strategy because it supports concepts in geometry, algebra, algorithms, and reasoning. Additionally, because of the level of focus, engagement, and time spent with the Rubik's Cube, students feel a sense of accomplishment when they solve certain parts or successfully complete steps in the process.

Some other mathematics games to consider include the following:

- **K–5:** The Math is Fun website (www.mathisfun.com) is ideal for use as a learning station or for classes with one-to-one device use. Games range from challenging mathematics classics, such as Sudoku, to counting exercises for younger students.
- **K–12:** The game Prodigy (www.prodigy.com) borrows elements from role-playing games such as Pokémon, as players compete in mathematics duels against in-game characters.

- **Grades 1–8:** In the game Around the Block, students use a ball to practice mathematics skills. Students solve mathematics tasks before passing the ball to the next person in the group.
- **Grades 3–8:** In the game Math Baseball, one team starts at bat, scoring runs by choosing questions worth one, two, or three bases. Students "pitch" the questions, which range in difficulty depending on how many bases they're worth. If the at-bat team answers incorrectly, the defending team can respond correctly to earn an out. After three outs, teams switch sides. Students play until one team gets ten runs.
- **Grades 6 and up:** The Get the Math website (www.thirteen.org/get-the-math) contains videos with young professionals who explain how they use mathematics in their fields, such as fashion design and video game development. Teachers can assign challenges to the class after watching, which involve playing games.

Academic games are quick remedies for disengagement and provide students with a fresh look at content. When using academic games, it is important to preserve inconsequential competition. Such competition takes place in the spirit of fun, teachers should change team composition periodically so that all students have the opportunity to be on a winning team, and any rewards associated with winning should be minimal. Figure 7.9 depicts the self-reflection scale for this element.

Score	Description
4: Innovating	I adapt behaviors and create new strategies for unique student needs and situations.
3: Applying	I use academic games and inconsequential competition to maintain student engagement, and I monitor the extent to which students focus on the academic content of the game.
2: Developing	I use academic games and inconsequential competition to maintain student engagement, but I do not monitor the effect on students.
1: Beginning	I use the strategies and behaviors associated with this element incorrectly or with parts missing.
0: Not Using	I am unaware of strategies and behaviors associated with this element.

Figure 7.9: Self-rating scale for element 30—Using academic games.

Element 31: Providing Opportunities for Students to Talk About Themselves

Marzano (2017) explains that when students perceive that they are welcome in class they will be more engaged in learning. One way to make them feel welcome is to provide opportunities for students to talk about themselves. But before students will talk about themselves, they must feel like they belong to a safe and trusted space. In *The New Art and Science of Teaching* framework, Marzano (2017) suggests teachers administer interest surveys that include goals, personal or family history, existing knowledge in the content area, and class expectations or desires. They can also collect information about students as part of learning profiles that specify students' preferred learning styles and how they learn best. Teachers can also make life connections between the content and students' own personal and life experiences, hobbies, and interests. With the strategy of informal linkages during class discussion, teachers relate class content to student interests and experiences. They must also feel like others are sincerely listening. A very important aspect of students talking about themselves is for them to become effective and active listeners. This will help students support those who are sharing and more effectively reflect on their own stories.

Carl R. Rogers and F. J. Roethlisberger (2014) theorize that when speakers feel that listeners are being empathic, attentive, and nonjudgmental, they relax and share their inner feelings and thoughts without worrying about what listeners will think of them. This safe discussion environment encourages speakers to dive deeper into their consciousness and discover new insights about themselves, even those that may challenge previously held beliefs and perceptions.

Guy Itzchakov and Avraham N. Kluger (2018) conducted a series of studies on the impact and power of active listening. In one of their studies, the researchers assigned undergraduate students to serve as either a speaker or a listener and paired them up, sitting face to face. They asked speakers to talk about their attitudes toward a specific subject. They instructed the listeners to "listen as you listen when you are at your best." But they randomly distracted half of the listeners by sending them text messages and instructed them to answer briefly, so the speakers saw that they were distracted. Afterward, they asked the speakers questions about whether they were worried about what their partner thought of them, whether they acquired any insight while talking, and whether they were confident in their beliefs. They found that speakers paired with good listeners felt less anxious, more self-aware, and stated higher clarity about their attitudes on the topics. Speakers paired with undistracted listeners also reported being more willing to share their attitude with others. They also found that high-quality listening helps speakers see both sides of an argument (called attitude complexity).

In another study, Itzchakov and Avraham (2018) find that speakers who conversed with a good listener reported attitudes that were more complex and less extreme—in other words, not one-sided. Putting all of their findings together, we conclude that good listening seems to make the speaker more relaxed, more self-aware of his or her strengths and weaknesses, and more willing to reflect in a nondefensive manner. These qualities of good listening can motivate students to more readily share their experiences and attitudes with other students.

The checklist in figure 7.10 supports students in becoming active listeners when other students are sharing their attitudes and beliefs.

- ☐ **Put away technology.** Phones, tablets, and laptops are distracting. The speaker must have 100 percent of the listener's attention.
- ☐ **Never interrupt.** Allow the speaker to talk and pause his or her speaking without asking questions or inserting our thoughts.
- ☐ **Save your solutions.** The listener's role is to truly engage with the speaker. Listeners should save for later all judgments and solutions, or never express them, depending on the learning opportunity.
- ☐ **Ask thoughtful questions.** When it is time to speak, ask questions to help the speaker think more deeply about his or her thoughts and experiences. Thoughtful questions may also help the speaker arrive at a solution, if that's what's intended.

Figure 7.10: Active listening checklist.

Visit **go.SolutionTree.com/instruction** *for a free reproducible version of this figure.*

To fully support student voices in the mathematics classroom, teachers must also develop the conditions in which these voices can be heard. When students share, they want their listeners to fully experience their perspective. This requires empathy, which educators must encourage in the mathematics classroom.

It can be a challenging endeavor to experience a deep sense of empathy, especially if one has not shared experiences similar to those of the speaker. Showing true empathy requires exploring why another person feels or experiences the world in a certain way.

Empathy isn't created by listeners guessing the speaker's intent or imagining what it's like to be in someone else's shoes. In fact, empathy starts when listeners stop guessing about what's on the mind of the speaker, and instead learn to actively listen.

Teachers can express empathy toward their students by asking students to share their thinking about mathematics frequently, such as during morning meetings or in closing circles. When a student shares his or her thinking and reasoning, he or she is expressing understanding on an intellectual level, as well as revealing in detail how he or she thinks and feels about a particular experience or concept. When students effectively share and listen, they are able to see others' perspectives.

There are four simple steps educators can employ to encourage active listening in the mathematics classroom and build empathy among their students.

1. Listen to the explanation the student is sharing.
2. Paraphrase the explanation the student just shared.
3. Receive confirmation from the student that the explanation has been perceived the way he or she intended.
4. Allow the explainer to reflect on the listeners' perspectives.

Figure 7.11 provides an example of an activity that follows this protocol.

---

1. Ask students to pair up. The explainer has three to five minutes to share his or her explanation.

2. Instruct students to use story starters, such as the following.
   - "Because this mathematics concept was challenging for me, I want to change my approach to dealing with frustrations by . . ."
   - "My teacher or fellow students pushed my thinking in the following way . . ."
   - "This was something risky I tried and it worked . . ."
   - "I think I have this quality or characteristic because of this experience I've been through . . ."

3. Tell listeners that they should remain silent until the speaker's time is up, and announce when time is up.

4. The listener summarizes the storyteller's message by restating the big idea and reflecting on his or her feelings when hearing the story. For example:
   - "So, I heard you saying . . ."
   - "This is what I understand to be your emotion about . . ."

5. The speaker then gives feedback about how it felt to have the listener actively listen. For example:
   - "I felt like I had something important to share when you gave cues that you were listening to me."
   - "I felt valued when you were focused on listening to my explanation."

Figure 7.11: Active listening protocol.

Active listening allows both the explainer and the listener to develop depth of understanding and provides a window into the storyteller's values, levels of thinking, emotions, and presuppositions behind their experiences.

When students have opportunities to talk about themselves in relation to academic content, it creates connections for them that are inherently engaging. Figure 7.12 depicts the self-reflection scale for this element.

Score	Description
4: Innovating	I adapt behaviors and create new strategies for unique student needs and situations.
3: Applying	I provide opportunities for students to talk about themselves, and I monitor the extent to which my actions affect students' engagement.
2: Developing	I provide opportunities for students to talk about themselves, but I do not monitor the effect on students.
1: Beginning	I use the strategies and behaviors associated with this element incorrectly or with parts missing.
0: Not Using	I am unaware of strategies and behaviors associated with this element.

Figure 7.12: Self-rating scale for element 31—Providing opportunities for students to talk about themselves.

GUIDING QUESTIONS FOR CURRICULUM DESIGN

This design question focuses on engagement: *What engagement strategies will I use to help students pay attention, be energized, be intrigued, and be inspired?* The following questions, which align to each of the elements in this chapter, guide teachers to plan instruction. Teachers would clearly not use all elements in a single unit of instruction but would frequently—if not daily—notice when students are disengaged or unresponsive, increase response rates, use physical movement, maintain a lively pace, and demonstrate intensity and enthusiasm. Consider the following questions aligned to the elements in this chapter to guide your planning.

- **Element 23:** What will I do to notice when students are not engaged and react?

  _____

  _____

  _____

  _____

  _____

  _____

- **Element 25:** What will I do to increase students' physical movement?

  _____

  _____

  _____

  _____

  _____

  _____

- **Element 28:** What will I do to present unusual information?

_____

_____

_____

_____

_____

- **Element 29:** What will I do to engage students in friendly controversy?

_____

_____

_____

_____

_____

- **Element 30:** What will I do to engage students in academic games?

_____

_____

_____

_____

_____

- **Element 31:** What will I do to provide opportunities for students to talk about themselves?

_____

_____

_____

_____

_____

_____

Summary

Using engagement strategies involves ten elements: (1) noticing and reacting when students are not engaged, (2) increasing response rates, (3) using physical movement, (4) maintaining a lively pace, (5) demonstrating intensity and enthusiasm, (6) presenting unusual information, (7) using friendly controversy, (8) using academic games, (9) providing opportunities for students to talk about themselves, (10) and motivating and inspiring students. This chapter covered six of the elements that connect strongly to engaging students in the mathematics classroom where teachers have a vast array of options to implement each element. Techniques such as those outlined in this chapter assist teachers in facilitating experiences that connect learners to mathematics content in a way that empowers them to become problem solvers, critical thinkers, and self-directed learners.

CHAPTER 8

Implementing Rules and Procedures

Rules and procedures have long been foundational to good instruction, regardless of the subject matter. However, how best to establish predictable and dependable modes of interaction between and among those inside a classroom has changed dramatically since the start of the 21st century. Prior to this time, school and districts emphasized teacher-centered classrooms in which control emanated from the front of the room. Now there has been a shift to a much more distributed form of classroom management in which students have a critical role in establishing and maintaining an orderly, efficient, and inviting environment.

There are five elements in the eighth design area of *The New Art and Science of Teaching*—implementing rules and procedures: establishing rules and procedures (element 33), organizing the physical layout of the classroom (element 34), demonstrating withitness (element 35), acknowledging adherence to rules and procedures (element 36), and acknowledging lack of adherence to rules and procedures (element 37).

In this chapter, we address the first two of these five elements: establishing rules and procedures (element 33) and organizing the physical layout of the classroom (element 34).

Element 33: Establishing Rules and Procedures

The shift from a teacher-centered classroom to a student-centered classroom does not imply that the role of the teacher has diminished; actually, the opposite is true. The role of the teacher in the classroom has never been so important. In any classroom, especially the mathematics classroom, the most successful learning occurs when the teacher is a facilitator or activator of learning. Instead of simply giving students sets of mathematics problems or assigning them mathematics drills, teachers are designing learning experiences that build on student strengths. This in turn empowers students to create new connections and more complex thinking by engaging with mathematics through real-life problem solving and perseverance.

Because of this instructional and professional shift, it's important that the teacher establish and communicate clear rules and procedures with students so as to set the stage for positive interactions and relationships between teacher and student and among students and peers.

From the start of the school year or when students first enroll in class, teachers should clarify students' expectations for the class (ask the students what they'd like to get from the class). This practice challenges conventional methods of instruction in which the teacher tells the students what to expect. It begins the process of students co-creating learning goals and addresses any anxiety or misconceptions that students have about the teacher, class, or mathematics in general. The most successful teacher-student relationships are ones built on safety, trust, and respect, and those in which the student fully understands and shares the teacher's vision for learning success.

Another important aspect in establishing rules and procedures is to provide a structure and frequency for communication and feedback with students and parents. In the past, teachers would communicate through grades, report cards, or phone calls to parents. But everyday feedback to students will provide more specific and helpful feedback and will lead to higher learning growth.

Nancy Frey and Douglas Fisher (2011) explain that feedback must be timely, understandable, and actionable. In the mathematics classroom, teachers give timely feedback through the problem-solving process, in small groups, and individually—and not just on assessments. This ensures students have time to act and implement the feedback through revision. The specific or understandable nature of feedback ensures students know exactly what parts of their reasoning needs revision or what parts of their solution path show inaccuracies. Actionable feedback ensures students can take an objective view of teacher or student feedback and immediately make changes. It's important that language isn't vague and that it doesn't just praise a student for a right answer. Affirmation is important, but it must be separate from feedback.

With feedback, for example, the teacher should establish a procedure so students know what to expect. If the class is working in an online collaborative document, will the teacher provide comments in the document itself, or will he or she use another LMS? How often will the teacher hold academic or learning conferences? These are structures that a teacher should explicitly communicate to students.

Finally, teachers must make it clear that responsibility is a critical guiding principle in the mathematics classroom. Teachers must communicate to students that this is non-negotiable. Students are responsible for their own learning, with teachers creating the best conditions for learning. If a student produces work that doesn't meet expectations, it's the responsibility of the teacher and the student to determine why it doesn't meet expectations (as measured by a rubric) and determine the plan for the student to revise work in order meet or exceed expectations. Responsible student behaviors include showing how they arrived at an answer, recording reflections, and bringing their reflections to meetings with the teacher, no matter what grade level.

Part of encouraging responsibility is making sure students feel valued in the mathematics classroom. That responsibility doesn't mean complying with rules, but rather an agreed-on operating principle because teachers want students to succeed in learning at the highest levels.

Mathematics learning and instruction are most effective when teachers have implemented nurturing and explicit structures to help students develop social skills, positive relationships, and positive decision-making skills. Self-management and positive decision making support students' well-being (emotions, attitudes, behaviors, and choices) and increase learning in mathematics (and all academics) (The Collaborative for Academic, Social, and Emotional Learning [CASEL], 2018).

Most teachers agree that high expectations are an integral part of the classroom. But communication of these expectations shouldn't be grounded in rules of compliance. What if we shift our communication from high expectations to inspiring aspirations? Carol S. Dweck (2007) explains that students are more intrinsically motivated if they're inspired to act in a way that exemplifies their identity through the process of learning, achieving, and reflecting. Effective praise should communicate that student actions (and the student making the positive choices) contribute to the greater good. Figure 8.1 provides a few examples of how mathematics teachers can begin to change their daily language with students. The left side includes statements that are teacher-centric—expectations based in compliance. The right side provides examples of how teachers could transform their communication to exemplify communication that encourages student aspirations.

Teacher-Centric Expectations	Student-Centric Aspirations
"I need everyone to close their laptops while I'm talking."	"How can we all get the most out of today's learning?"
"I need your math problems completed before we begin the project."	"Do you have everything you need to prepare for our project his afternoon?"
"Next time, make sure you isolate *x* before dividing."	"Did you understand why you were solving the math problem this way?"
"I'm not seeing growth in your behavior. We might need to put you in another classroom during rotations."	"We are a classroom of learners, and we're all in this learning journey together. How are you feeling about current challenges and struggles?"
"I need you to come prepared to our academic conference."	"I'm going to record my reflections daily so I can accurately capture everything surrounding the goals we've created together. I'm looking forward to hearing your reflection on the choices you are making."

Figure 8.1: Transforming expectations to aspirations.

Notice that the aspirational statements on the right are not as direct as the statements on the left, but instead they serve as prompts. Framing rules and procedures into aspiring questions places the action solely on the student, instead of a directive from the teacher, allowing students the opportunity to act out of desire and purpose. The standards for mathematical practice (NGA & CCSSO, 2010) call for students to make sense of problems and persevere through them. Aspirational statements help students take control of their own learning, which includes sense making.

Mathematics teachers can implement morning meetings and mathematics activities to support social skills and responsible decision making to support student-centric classrooms.

Morning Meeting

Begin each day by establishing a strong sense of camaraderie and community in the mathematics classroom, which ensures that students will be the most successful in their learning space. Responsive Classroom (2016) suggests a gathering time every morning lasting twenty to thirty minutes called morning meeting. According to the Responsive Classroom morning meeting format, teachers and students interact purposefully using the following four components.

1. **Greeting:** Students and teachers greet one another by name.
2. **Sharing:** Students share information about important events in their lives. The listening students are encouraged to offer empathetic responses or ask clarifying questions.
3. **Group activity:** Everyone participates in a brief, lively activity that fosters group cohesion and helps students practice social and academic skills (for example, rapping a mathematics song).
4. **Morning message:** Students read and interact with a short inspiring message written by their teacher. The message is crafted to help students aspire to focus on the upcoming work and learning they'll be doing.

Morning meeting activities support a growth mindset for tackling mathematics problems or reviewing the previous day's mathematics concepts. Mathematics can induce stress or frustration for some students; therefore, introducing it into morning meetings creates a more casual and collaborative atmosphere for solving mathematics problems. Morning meeting is a great place to make real-world connections to mathematics, to encourage students to explain their thinking, practice respectful conversations and debates, and remind students why they are solving mathematics problems. At the intermediate and secondary levels, morning meetings can be those first few minutes of the class period or learning block. Figure 8.2 presents an example of a mathematics activity that could be a part of building number sense. The example would work well in elementary and intermediate grades. For secondary grades, you could use algebraic expression in the script or even fractions for those students struggling with fundamental algebraic concepts.

Description:

Stand in a circle with a ball in your hand. The class will provide a number, and the teacher is going to call out a different number. The group's job is to figure out how the teacher is changing the numbers (the teacher applies the same change each time).

Script:

Toss the ball to a student, who will say, "I give you _____," and toss the ball back to the teacher. The teachers says back, "I give you _____." (An alternate wording could be, "In goes _____" and "Out comes _____.") For example, perhaps you have decided that the function will be "add five." You toss the ball to a student, who says "I give you ten," and then tosses the ball back to the teacher. The teacher says, "I give you fifteen."

Parameter:

Students must wait until three exchanges have occurred before offering a guess at the change you're making, even if they suspect they know the change.

Reflection:

Ask the students to explain their thinking in how they figured out the formula.

Figure 8.2: Ball-toss mathematics patterns game.

Activities to Support Social Skills and Responsible Decision Making

Active engagement in mathematics (and in all academic and non-academic areas as well) hinges on students' ability to make positive choices while understanding how their choices align with social norms. Students, as effective collaborators and good classroom citizens, recognize there are many ways to solve problems or reason through new scenarios, and they understand that the methods of fellow students can help them identify new ways of thinking and learning. Empathetic discourse and active listening are critical skills when applying mathematical reasoning. These should be expectations and part of rules and procedures in the mathematics classroom.

Following is a list of activities that can support responsible decision making, self-management, and relationship building.

- Read fictional stories (for examples, *A Wrinkle in Time* by Madeleine L'Engle, *The Number Devil* by Hans Magnus Enzensberger, and *Flatland* by Edwin A. Abbott) about characters who use mathematics in clever ways to solve problems, or discuss how mathematics savants (such as Pythagoras, Sir Isaac Newton, Albert Einstein, and so on) or novices persevered through challenges and difficulties to make a significant mathematical discovery. Based on facts and inferences, how did these people feel while solving problems, and why did they solve problems in a particular way? Ask students to reflect on how they feel when faced with mathematics challenges.

- Ask students to identify their own personal hobbies, interests, strengths, and weaknesses in general. Then ask students to use visual representations to quantify these characteristics (for example, "Draw a scatter plot of the positive interactions you had today" or "Create a pie chart to show your strength levels in a particular skill.")
- Provide praise and affirmation to students when they persevere through problems. Give authentic feedback when students persevere (such as, "When you had difficulty solving the polynomial equation, you then tried the array strategy and were successful at finding a solution. Your perseverance resulted in success!" or "When you were unclear on the directions, you asked a friend instead of disengaging. Asking for help instead of giving up will get you far in life!")
- Tell stories about famous mathematics savants who showed respect for each other within a specific area of expertise (such as Blaise Pascal and Pierre de Fermat, or create a theoretical friendly debate on the theory of gravity between Isaac Newton and Albert Einstein as if they had lived in the same time period). Use examples of communication between thinkers to show how to have friendly debates without feelings getting hurt or people feeling criticized.
- Routinely ask students to discuss issues that matter to them and how they would create solutions. This group discussion sheds light on differing student worldviews, personalities, and backgrounds and how they have similar or different preferences. Students learn from each other about why other concepts and problem-solving approaches are interesting.
- Use project-based learning experiences that draw on mathematics mindsets and skills. A part of collaboration is students deciding as a small group how they will work together. This discussion prompts students to answer questions about how they best work in a group and illuminates their individual collaborative skills.
- Encourage students to reflect on how they approached mathematics that day. Morning meetings or closing circles (the beginning or ending of class for intermediate and secondary students) are excellent uses of time for reflection. Or students can individually reflect in their journals. Ask students to talk about risks they took that were successful or failures that they want to improve on.

These engagement procedures create the intrinsic motivation to follow co-established rules and routines. Establishing rules and procedures plays a key role in promoting order or the lack of it in the classroom. Figure 8.3 depicts the self-reflection scale for this element.

Score	Description
4: Innovating	I adapt behaviors and create new strategies for unique student needs and situations.
3: Applying	I establish rules and procedures, and I monitor the extent to which my actions affect students' behavior.
2: Developing	I establish rules and procedures, but I do not monitor the effect on students.
1: Beginning	I use the strategies and behaviors associated with this element incorrectly or with parts missing.
0: Not Using	I am unaware of strategies and behaviors associated with this element.

Figure 8.3: Self-rating scale for element 33—Establishing rules and procedures.

Element 34: Organizing the Physical Layout of the Classroom

Learning flourishes when teachers create a calm, yet engaging learning environment that promotes a good balance of structure and autonomy. A well-organized learning space sends students a powerful and positive message: this space was designed specifically for you, with your specific needs in mind, because you and your learning are important.

Changing the classroom configuration or changing to newer, soft seating doesn't inherently promote a change in student learning dispositions or behaviors. Before changing the physical learning space, teachers must have clear goals and outcomes in mind about how they want learning or behaviors to change as a result of the environment.

Following are some ideas for strategies presented in *The New Art and Science of Teaching* for creating a physical environment that makes students feel comfortable and significant and that best serves the needs of all students.

- Create learning centers or areas of the classroom for group work that are specifically for fun and discovery, such as an area with Legos, Play-Doh, robotics, and so on (these engage students of all levels). Creative and unstructured play can reinforce many mathematics skills (such as problem solving, reasoning, and justification).
- Provide flexibility in how students work and make thinking visible when considering classroom materials and technology equipment. Use multiple options for presentation (videos, slides, stand and deliver, group presentations, and so on) and multiple means of expression (written, narrative, spoken, visual, and so on).
- In areas for group work and centers, encourage students to use multisensory objects to build learning, such as mathematics manipulatives, mathematics apps, sound-enabled apps (apps that are receptive to sound input), mathematics videos, writing stations (with tactile connections involving drawing or writing about the mathematics), and so on.
- When designing classroom décor, include natural lighting in the classroom (open the blinds or rearrange seating so it is close to windows), and add paint to the walls to give it a casual, fun, and vibrant look and feel.
- When placing student desks, include lighter, softer, and more flexible seating that allows for quick transitions and more effective use of strategies (such as fishbowls, Socratic seminars, group projects, independent time, and so on).

The physical environment of the classroom can help stimulate a sense of order or lack of it. Figure 8.4 depicts the self-reflection scale for this element.

Score	Description
4: Innovating	I adapt behaviors and create new strategies for unique student needs and situations.
3: Applying	I organize the physical layout of the classroom, and I monitor the extent to which my actions affect students' behavior.
2: Developing	I organize the physical layout of the classroom, but I do not monitor the effect on students.
1: Beginning	I use the strategies and behaviors associated with this element incorrectly or with parts missing.
0: Not Using	I am unaware of strategies and behaviors associated with this element.

Figure 8.4: Self-rating scale for element 34—Organizing the physical layout of the classroom.

GUIDING QUESTIONS FOR CURRICULUM DESIGN

The design question in this chapter focuses on implementing rules and procedures: *What strategies will I use to help students understand and follow rules and procedures?* Consider the following questions aligned to the elements in this chapter to guide your planning.

- **Element 33:** What will I do to establish rules and procedures in the classroom?

_____

_____

_____

_____

_____

_____

_____

_____

- **Element 34:** What will I do to make the physical layout of the classroom most conducive to learning?

_____

_____

_____

_____

_____

_____

_____

_____

_____

_____

Summary

Implementing rules and procedures involves establishing them in the classroom and organizing the physical layout of the classroom. In the mathematics classroom, rules and procedures are best implemented in a positive learning environment and with the teacher developing positive routines alongside the students, as described in this chapter.

CHAPTER 9

Building Relationships

The ninth design area of *The New Art and Science of Teaching* framework involves creating a classroom context in which students feel welcome, accepted, and valued. In a community with high levels of relational trust, students can focus their attention on the content at hand. A common trap when thinking about relationships in the classroom is to focus on the relationship between teacher and students. While this is certainly an important relationship, equally, if not more important, is the relationships students have with one another. Consequently, teachers must aim strategies for building relationships at helping students feel welcome, accepted, and valued by the teacher and their peers.

Teachers can create a classroom atmosphere that helps build positive relationships by appropriately using verbal and nonverbal behaviors that indicate affection for students (element 38), understanding students' backgrounds and interests (element 39), and adhering to personal standards of behavior that communicate and display objectivity and control (element 40). In this chapter, we address the final two elements, understanding students' backgrounds and interests (element 39) and displaying objectivity and control (element 40) within the context of the mathematics classroom.

Element 39: Understanding Students' Backgrounds and Interests

Challenges around managing student behavior exist because teachers tend to focus on how they themselves would behave in certain situations and why; they often assume students share their value system. Teachers may ask, "How can I get my student to change this behavior?" Instead of focusing on changing the student, however, teachers should shift focus to how teacher actions connect to students' motivation. The question teachers should ask then becomes, "What can I do to support my student to change this behavior?"

For example, some students may possess a higher sense of freedom to express their reasoning processes than other students based on their specific values or worldviews (for example, some students are allowed to challenge authority figures in their home). Or other students might choose one strategy over another or embrace an innovative approach based on their life experiences and backgrounds (some students prefer to doodle and already choose to visually represent mathematics solutions). Most educators understand the value of differentiated instruction because students learn in different ways. They must also apply this same understanding to facilitating positive student behavior. The following strategies help teachers understand students' backgrounds and interests.

- Endeavor to understand how individual learners think, learn, and adapt to change by offering students multiple ways to solve problems and multiple ways to express their thinking (visually, orally, tactilely, and so on). Change requires evolution, and, therefore, teachers must create innovative ways to support student learning based on who they have become in the midst of new circumstances. Once a teacher recognizes a student flourishes in one learning modality, he or she should help students build this strength. For example, if a student thrives while making videos of mathematics explanations, then allow students to use this modality to solve mathematics problems.
- Facilitate students making meaningful connections with one another. Connecting familiar, everyday concepts of shopping, building, measuring, planning, designing, and so on to mathematics content facilitates these connections.
- Facilitate students making meaningful connections with instructional strategies, learning experiences, and technology tools.
- Provide students with differentiated and varied ways of thinking and options for how they can create different solution paths and innovative approaches to solving mathematics problems.

Understanding students' backgrounds and interests goes a long way in developing positive relationships between teacher and students and among peers. Figure 9.1 depicts the self-reflection scale for this element so teachers can gauge their performance.

Score	Description
4: Innovating	I adapt behaviors and create new strategies for unique student needs and situations.
3: Applying	I understand students' backgrounds and interests, and I monitor the extent to which my actions affect students.
2: Developing	I understand students' backgrounds and interests, but I do not monitor the effect on students.
1: Beginning	I use the strategies and behaviors associated with this element incorrectly or with parts missing.
0: Not Using	I am unaware of strategies and behaviors associated with this element.

Figure 9.1: Self-rating scale for element 39—Understanding students' backgrounds and interests.

Element 40: Displaying Objectivity and Control

Nathan Lang-Raad (2018) explains how implicit biases also have an enormous impact on both personal behavior and relationships within the school. Biases affect decisions educators make about student potential and managing student behavior. Ohio State University's Kirwan Institute for the Study of Race and Ethnicity (2015) defines implicit bias as follows:

> Implicit bias refers to the attitudes or stereotypes that affect our understanding, actions, and decisions in an unconscious manner. These biases, which encompass both favorable and unfavorable assessments, are activated involuntarily and without an individual's awareness or intentional control.

To create positive relationships with students, teachers must take purposeful steps to create inclusive class-rooms. In *Everyday Bias*, Howard J. Ross (2014) provides a framework of systems and structures that illumi-nate bias patterns and provide remedies to address them to promote an open exchange of diverse ideas. He provides a strategy using the mnemonic PAUSE as shown in figure 9.2.

P: Pay attention to what's actually happening beneath the judgments and assessments.

A: Acknowledge your own reactions, interpretations, and judgments.

U: Understand the other reactions, interpretations, and judgments that may be possible.

S: Search for the most constructive, empowering, or productive way to deal with the situation.

E: Execute your action plan.

Source: Ross, 2014.

Figure 9.2: The PAUSE strategy.

*Visit **go.SolutionTree.com/instruction** for a free reproducible version of this figure.*

Consider a scenario in which you have an academic conference with a student about his or her progress with a respective mathematics concept. You notice that the student looks down frequently and exhibits minimal eye contact. Figure 9.3 applies the PAUSE strategy to such a scenario.

Scenario: During a conference, a student looks down frequently and makes limited eye contact.
P: Pay attention to what's actually happening beneath the judgments and assessments.
What's actually happening is that the student doesn't look me in the eye for the same amount of time that I look others in the eye—he is, however, making some eye contact.
A: Acknowledge your own reactions, interpretations, and judgments.
My initial interpretation is that the student possesses low self-esteem or self-confidence or he is insecure with his ability to communicate about the mathematics concept.
U: Understand the other reactions, interpretations, and judgments that may be possible.
Is the student intimidated by my body language, my use of eye contact, or my ability to effectively communicate about his learning? Does this student simply prefer to communicate without sustained eye contact? Does this student come from a different cultural background?
S: Search for the most constructive, empowering, or productive way to deal with the situation.
I'll continue to speak in a student-friendly, informal, and casual tone, staying cognizant of my eye contact and varying the duration of my eye contact to ensure the student feels open and willing about sharing his learning reflections.
E: Execute your action plan.
I will continue to get to know this student and foster a classroom environment of trust and transparency, taking note as student behaviors and dispositions change.

Figure 9.3: PAUSE example scenario.

Using the PAUSE strategy encourages teachers to look at all the possibilities to help disarm their immediate and potentially wrong conclusions about students. By illuminating natural inclinations when conversing with students and making proactive changes in their own actions, teachers can better display objectivity and control, contributing to the creation of a safe and nurturing culture in which equity prevails.

Besides the PAUSE strategy, there are additional actions teachers can take to address bias head-on, proactively engage diversity (celebrate our differences), and disengage subjectivity (be aware of biases based on personal experiences). Use the strategy of student background surveys to learn about students' academic interests, personal interests, dreams, fears, family members, and family activities.

- **Create a list of unstructured processes and structure them:** What activities do you do that don't align to a specific purpose or process? Consider, for example, the students you call on frequently to help with jobs around the classroom or question often during whole-group instruction. What leads you to call on certain students more? Do they display similar personality traits? Are they more amenable to classroom duties? Do you interact equally with all ethnic groups in the school? Do you tend to give more praise to certain students, regardless of the evidence you collect? Also, consider your feedback system. Have you structured it to align to previously established goals, or have you based it on your own presuppositions about students? Once you develop your list of unstructured processes, create an unbiased structure. Ensure your daily interactions include all students. Create feedback processes that align with co-created goals. Structure allows teachers to make sure that all students have opportunities to be nurtured, embraced, and successful so they can grow. For example, provide a structure to ensure teachers are giving feedback to students as they solve tasks (addressing gaps in student thinking or student misconceptions).

- **Have daily conversations with all students and actively listen:** Diversity doesn't just refer to demographic differences such as gender, race, and socioeconomic background; it also includes thinking style, personality, and learning modalities. These conversations can be about favorite mathematics projects or challenges students have learned the most from. Educators can only understand the latter by actively listening to students to understand their perspectives. Personally and professionally, we have observed that the more teachers get to know a student, the more differences emerge; teachers can embrace these differences to everyone's benefit.

- **Encourage dissenters to speak out:** Students who are eager to communicate dissenting views can often frustrate teachers—especially when teachers believe that students should think, learn, and behave in specific ways. A determining factor in student growth in mathematical problem solving and reasoning is the ability to communicate alternative ways to solve problems. Are there students in your class who disagree with you often or try to derail your efforts? For example, do students derail your efforts to show multiple pathways to a solution, especially if they've discovered a solution that they like? Give those students the opportunity to reason through their thinking by having thoughtful, reflective dialogues in a safe, nurturing classroom environment.

Displaying objectivity and control involves the teacher staying calm in potentially agitating situations. Figure 9.4 depicts the self-reflection scale for this element so teachers can gauge their performance.

Score	Description
4: Innovating	I adapt behaviors and create new strategies for unique student needs and situations.
3: Applying	I display objectivity and control, and I monitor the extent to which my actions affect students.
2: Developing	I display objectivity and control, but I do not monitor the effect on students.
1: Beginning	I use the strategies and behaviors associated with this element incorrectly or with parts missing.
0: Not Using	I am unaware of strategies and behaviors associated with this element.

Figure 9.4: Self-rating scale for element 40—Displaying objectivity and control.

GUIDING QUESTIONS FOR CURRICULUM DESIGN

The design question in this chapter focuses on building relationships: *What strategies will I use to I help students feel welcome, accepted, and valued?* The following questions, which align to each of the elements in this chapter, guide teachers to plan rules and build relationships.

- **Element 39:** What strategies will I use to demonstrate that I understand students' backgrounds and interests?

_____

_____

_____

_____

_____

_____

_____

_____

- **Element 40:** What strategies will I use to demonstrate objectivity and control?

_____

_____

_____

_____

_____

_____

_____

_____

Summary

Building relationships involves understanding students' backgrounds and interests and displaying objectivity and control. In the mathematics classroom, cultural characteristics have the potential to impact relationships both positively and negatively. Teachers should evaluate their interactions with students to assess whether or not they experience bias and adjust their actions accordingly. Teachers must also acknowledge that what students feel, think, and believe about learning shifts and changes as they grow and learn. As students' values change, so should teacher actions. Mathematics teachers who acknowledge, appreciate, and leverage this knowledge can smooth the path toward safe, trusting relationships with their students.

CHAPTER 10

Creating High Expectations

The tenth and final design area of *The New Art and Science of Teaching* framework is communicating high expectations. Our discussion in this chapter focuses on the reluctant learner. Often the low expectations of teachers go hand in hand with reluctance on the part of students. This is an unfortunate relationship but nonetheless a common one.

Teachers can form beliefs about students' chances of performing well academically. If the teacher forms a perception that a student will probably do well academically, the teacher treats that student in certain ways that encourage deep learning. If the teacher forms a perception that a student will probably not do well, the teacher doesn't interact with the student in ways that foster deep learning.

This scenario plays out with little or no conscious awareness on the part of the teacher or the students. The result is that those students for whom a teacher harbors low expectations become reluctant to engage in classroom activities—particularly those that are challenging. Additionally, the reluctant students will shy away from seeking out the very type of help that will produce the most rigorous learning.

Teachers can halt this cycle by examining their tacit beliefs about students and noticing any ways they might treat some students as less capable than others.

Specific patterns of interaction, questioning, and responding (highlighted in the elements of this design area) can help typically reluctant leaners feel valued and eager to interact with both the teacher and their peers. Teachers must use strategies for demonstrating value and respect for reluctant learners (element 41), asking in-depth questions of reluctant learners (element 42), and probing incorrect answers with reluctant learners (element 43).

Element 41: Demonstrating Value and Respect for Reluctant Learners

In the mathematics classroom, as in any classroom, it is important for teachers to hold high expectations for all students. The first step toward demonstrating equal value and respect for all students is to identify pre-existing differences in student expectations. Teachers must also strive to be aware of how their expectations and treatment of reluctant learners differs from other learners. A strategy for doing so is for a teacher to track his or her behavior for several days with a focus on tone and quality of interactions. However, when high expectations pair with a culture of compliance, a fear-based system can develop in which students pretend to be learners (there is no intrinsic motivation) in order to avoid consequences. In such an environment, students display behaviors and take actions they believe the teacher will find favorable. Because they don't have the freedom to make the choice to express independent ideas, students seek to gain praise and affirmation by blindly following rules.

When teacher expectations are highly relational, multidirectional, clear, continual, and growth centered, a classroom culture of genuine and authentic learning experiences can develop. In chapter 8, we shared how teachers can turn rules and procedures into more intrinsically motivating aspirations. By reconceptualizing expectations into shared inspirational statements, teachers create opportunities to communicate that they value to students, show they care about their challenges and frustrations, and assure them they are willing to put in the time and support necessary to learn and find solutions alongside them.

Expectations should not be rote, one-sided communication from the teacher. They should be agreed on and have value that resonates with students. Communicating expectations laced with purpose means recognizing and affirming students in meaningful, frequent, and consistent ways for actions that have real value. According to Dweck (2007), what people think about their own intelligence has a marked influence on their motivation to learn. A growth mindset exists when people believe they can develop their intelligence. Those with a *fixed mindset* think of intelligence as being an unchangeable quality that one either has or does not have. Dweck (2007) concludes that when educators praise students for "how smart you are in math," it doesn't increase motivation and resilience toward mathematics but instead encourages a fixed mindset. In contrast, praising students for the effort they put forth and how they process learning (through engagement, perseverance, strategy, improvement, and the like) promotes sustainable motivation. It tells students what they've done to succeed and what they need to do to succeed again in the future. Imagine a mathematics classroom full of students who have a desire to continually learn, grow, and experience mathematics success inside and outside of school.

Teachers can model a growth mindset by learning new skills and acquiring new knowledge alongside students. Teachers should highlight their own failures as they happen (when performing a think-aloud while solving a mathematics problem, for example), and focus on how they learned from those experiences.

Teachers can communicate positive, high expectations to students by providing sincere praise and affirmation. This seems easy enough to do for students who love school and learning. But all students must experience this acceptance, especially students who are reluctant to learn or those students who claim "math isn't my thing."

Traditional mathematics classrooms tend to focus on speed and drill exercises. Teachers must undo this misconception that mathematics must always be quickly learned and applied.

Kaustubh Supekar and colleagues (2013) note that the speed at which students appear to grasp mathematics concepts is not indicative of their mathematics potential. Students may give up early or not give careful attention to mathematics operations because they have determined they are not good at mathematics (they have a fixed mindset). Communicating high expectations (wrapped in inspiring language) can help students excel in mathematics no matter what their prior perceptions or experiences have been in the classroom.

In a responsive classroom environment, teachers combine high expectations with emotional support and affirmation. In a study by Rimm-Kaufman, Baroody, Larsen, Curby, and Abry (2014), researchers found that students who attended mathematics classrooms with higher emotional support reported increased engagement in mathematics learning. For example, in the study, fifth graders from emotionally supportive mathematics classrooms stated they were willing to exert more effort to understand the mathematics lesson. They enjoyed thinking about and solving problems in mathematics and were more willing to help peers learn new concepts. In another study by Gary W. Ladd, Sondra H. Birch, and Eric S. Buhs (1999), kindergarteners reported liking school more and experiencing less loneliness if they had a close relationship with their teachers. Furthermore, kindergarteners with better teacher—student relationships showed better performance on measures of early academic skills.

Figure 10.1 depicts the self-reflection scale for this element so teachers can gauge their performance.

Score	Description
4: Innovating	I adapt behaviors and create new strategies for unique student needs and situations.
3: Applying	I exhibit behaviors that demonstrate value and respect for reluctant learners, and I monitor the impact on students.
2: Developing	I exhibit behaviors that demonstrate value and respect for reluctant learners, but I do not monitor the effect on students.
1: Beginning	I use the strategies and behaviors associated with this element incorrectly or with parts missing.
0: Not Using	I am unaware of strategies and behaviors associated with this element.

Figure 10.1: Self-rating scale for element 41—Demonstrating value and respect for reluctant learners.

Element 42: Asking In-Depth Questions of Reluctant Learners

Teachers can help students become successful problem solvers with confidence in mathematics not by telling them what to do or how to act but instead by asking questions through inquiry-based instruction. Warren Berger (2014), an innovation expert and author of the book *A More Beautiful Question*, explains that one of the most powerful forces for inspiring change (in student behavior) and in daily life is a simple tool that we inherently have in all of us: questioning (or inquiry). Inquiry helps illuminate problems for students. A purposeful approach to inquiry combined with curiosity can inspire students during the learning process and help them create solutions and innovative ideas. Traditionally, teachers reward students for right answers instead of affirming students for asking challenging questions. This must change if teachers want to support creative problem solvers, especially for learners who might have moments of reluctance.

Two tools teachers can use to foster student questions include (1) the Question Formulation Technique and (2) inquiry circles, which we discuss in the following sections. These fit within the questioning strategies in *The New Art and Science of Teaching* framework.

Question Formulation Technique

Researchers Dan Rothstein, Luz Santana, and Andrew Minigan (2015) of the Right Question Institute (RQI) developed the Question Formulation Technique (QFT) process to help teachers provide students with both a structure for and the opportunity to practice generating and working with their own questions. By going through the steps of the process, students learn to think about their thinking. Using the QFT process can give teachers perspective on the attitudes and beliefs students hold about mathematics in general or with a specific mathematics concept. Teachers may find this process particularly useful at the beginning of a unit or when they notice a student struggling with the motivation to persevere.

Additionally, the QFT process works to develop students' questioning and inquiry-building skills, and supports them in becoming deeper thinkers. Once teachers develop the skill of inquiry through the QFT process, they should facilitate this process with students to help them understand a mathematics concept they are struggling with or to inspire motivation. The QFT process involves the following seven steps (Right Question Institute, n.d.).

1. Identifying a question focus
2. Following the rules for producing questions
   a. Ask as many questions as you can.
   b. Do not stop to discuss, judge, or answer any questions.
   c. Write down every question exactly as it is stated.
   d. Change any statement into a question.
3. Producing questions: Ask questions about the focus.
4. Improving questions
   a. Review your list of questions, and mark the open-ended questions with an *O* and the closed-ended questions with a *C*.
   b. Name the advantages and disadvantages of asking closed-ended questions.
   c. Name the advantages and disadvantages of asking open-ended questions.
   d. Change one closed-ended question into an open-ended question, and change one open-ended question into a closed-ended one.
5. Prioritizing questions
   a. Choose the three most important questions from your list. Mark them with an *X*.
   b. For what reasons did you select those three?
6. Establishing next steps: How will you use your questions?
7. Reflecting
   a. What did you learn? Record your reflections.
   b. What is the value of what you learned? Record your reflections.

Figure 10.2 shows an example of how the QFT process could unfold in the mathematics classroom.

Step 1: Identifying a Question Focus

Quote: Every math task in class should develop your mathematical thinking.

Step 2: Following the Rules for Producing Questions

1. Ask as many questions as you can.
2. Do not stop to discuss, judge, or answer any questions.
3. Write down every question exactly as it is stated.
4. Change any statement into a question.

The teacher asks, "What does this mean to you?"

Problems I solve shouldn't be about a series of steps to memorize. They should be about me thinking hard about every question and the possible paths to getting a solution.

Step 3: Producing Questions

Ask questions about the focus.

- *How do I discern when I'm engaging in mathematical thinking?*
- *Is memorizing helpful?*
- *Is memorizing easier?*
- *Do I feel prepared to think at a high level?*
- *How do I decide to do the things I do when I solve problems?*
- *Do I have an accurate picture of the results I get?*

- *How can I measure my mathematical thinking?*
- *Do my actions relate back to something I've been taught?*
- *How do I turn my past errors and mistakes into success today?*
- *Why do I resist mathematical thinking?*

Step 4: Improving Questions

Closed-ended questions can be answered with "yes" or "no" or another one-word response.

Open-ended questions require an explanation and cannot be answered with "yes" or "no" or another one-word response.

a. Review your list of questions, and mark the open-ended questions with an *O* and the closed-ended questions with a *C*.

- *How do I discern when I'm engaging in mathematical thinking? O*
- *Is memorizing helpful? C*
- *Is memorizing easier? C*
- *Do I feel prepared to think at a high level? C*
- *How do I decide to do the things I do when I solve problems? O*
- *Do I have an accurate picture of the results I get? C*
- *How can I measure my mathematical thinking? O*
- *Do my actions relate back to something I've been taught? C*
- *How do I turn my past errors and mistakes into success today? O*
- *Why do I resist mathematical thinking? O*

b. Name the advantages and disadvantages of asking closed-ended questions.

Advantages	Disadvantages
• *They promote clarity.* • *They are quick and easy to generate.* • *You use lower-level thinking to answer them.* • *More people have the ability to generate them.*	• *They are excessively simplistic; most complex questions can't be answered with a simple "yes" or "no."* • *They may not fully represent real-world thinking or scenarios.*

c. Name the advantages and disadvantages of asking open-ended questions.

Advantages	Disadvantages
• *They allow you to develop multiple answers and solutions.* • *They promote critical and divergent thinking and creativity.* • *They can help spawn more complex questions that get to the crux of a matter.*	• *They take longer to generate.* • *Variance in solutions could create ambiguity.*

d. Change one closed-ended question into an open-ended question, and change one open-ended question into a closed-ended one.

- *Is memorizing helpful? (C) changes to (O) Why do I find memorizing more helpful than reasoning through a problem?*
- *How do I decide to do the things I do when I solve problems? (O) changes to (C) What strategies has my teacher taught me when I solve problems?*

Figure 10.2: Example of the QFT process for mathematics.

continued →

Step 5: Prioritizing Questions

a. Choose the three most important questions from your list. Mark them with an X (or write them).

- *How do I decide to do the things I do when I solve problems?*
- *Why do I resist mathematical thinking?*
- *How can I measure my mathematical thinking?*

b. For what reasons did you select those three?

The questions I've chosen represent questions that will most challenge my thinking, and push me to think mathematically instead of memorizing steps.

Step 6: Establishing Next Steps

How will you use your questions?

I will use these questions to remind me of how important it is to approach every problem with an open mind, discovering the best path to a solution, and to think about my thinking along the way.

Step 7: Reflecting

a. What did you learn? Record your reflections.

I learned that many of the activities and tasks I do in math, I tend to approach with "what trick or series of steps have I memorized to get the right answer" instead of approaching the problem as an opportunity to share my thinking and reason through it.

b. What is the value of what you learned? Record your reflections.

Math should be about developing thinking and problem-solving skills, and not about memorizing steps.

Visit **go.SolutionTree.com/instruction** for a free reproducible version of this figure.

The inquiry process promotes self-direction for any learner (students and teachers) as the learner readily creates and revises his or her own questions and dives into concepts that truly have relevance to his or her work.

Following are some relevant questions for students to consider.

- How does my mindset affect my effort in mathematics?
- How does my mindset affect others?
- How does my mindset cause me to see the classroom differently?
- How does my mindset change the cycle of thinking and learning?
- How does my mindset connect mathematics concepts with my experiences, actions, and behaviors?
- How can I ask better questions to help learning become more meaningful?

Following are some relevant questions for mathematics teachers to consider.

- How does instruction affect my students' thinking and learning in meaningful ways?
- How does my role cause students to see the classroom differently?
- How does the struggle in the teaching profession deepen my own thinking about instruction and learning?

The QFT method is similar to the Socratic seminar strategy, which asks students to think deeply about a subject through questioning rather than the teacher giving students the content didactically. QFT turns that dynamic around and asks students to come up with the questions.

Inquiry Circles

Creating thoughtful questions for inquiry supports students in becoming more engaged mathematics learners. Betty Bisplinghoff (2017) developed the inquiry circles protocol to assist teachers in developing a deeper sense of inquiry. We have adapted it for use with students in the mathematics classroom (see figure 10.3 and figure 10.4, page 111). Teachers can use the protocol to generate questions about a mathematics project or challenge with the goal of exploring how students are thinking about mathematics, their frustrations, any challenges they are facing, and successes they've experienced along the way. The protocol has students sharing their mathematics stories, which supports and affirms their progress. Additionally, and especially with mathematics, students often feel as though they are the only ones who are experiencing frustrations. This process facilitates a student-to-student connection that starts to give new meaning to learning mathematics together. Teachers can best use the protocol as a reflection exercise, although they can also use it to transition to a new mathematics concept that connects to a closely related, previously learned concept.

Phase 1: Storytelling

1. Give students time (fifteen minutes) to reflect on their learning in their journal. It may be helpful to advise students to begin by listing recollections about good things in their work and then choose one item on that list to explore in more detail through drawing or writing. The following prompts can nudge this kind of thinking.
   - Think about times in this mathematics project when you felt like you were successful. List some of those successful moments.
   - Select one of those moments to write or draw about this successful experience.

2. When students complete their reflective writing, they move to fill an empty seat in the "circle of inquiry" (two circular grouping of chairs with one circle inside the other, chairs facing each other). Partner pairs are the students sitting knee-to-knee (one in the outer circle and one in the inner circle).

3. Students initiate the collaborative inquiry process by telling stories based on their written reflections. Partners will take turns telling and documenting the stories (thirty minutes total; fifteen minutes for each partner). What can prove to be most helpful to each storyteller and listener are the words and phrases that emerge during the storytelling as well as key concepts, themes, and ideas.
   - The storyteller talks for fifteen minutes.
   - The listener records notes, capturing important features of the story being shared.
   - The partner pairs switch roles for the next fifteen minutes.

4. Each student reviews the notes he or she took during the partner's story (ten minutes). This is preparation for retelling the partner's story in phase 2 of the protocol.

Phase 2: Retelling Approximately

1. Reconfigure the inside and outside circle pairings into two sets of partner pairs; in other words, pair up everyone in the inside circle and also in the outside circle.

2. Follow and then repeat each of the following steps for every person in the group (ten minutes per person, forty minutes total).
   - The partner (the one who listened to the story in the previous phase) introduces the storyteller to the group and retells the story that he or she heard (four minutes).
   - The storyteller has time to add to or clarify what his or her partner has shared (two minutes). The storyteller uses this time to confirm the highlights his or her partner shared and add any other necessary details.

3. The group members ask clarifying questions (four minutes). It is helpful to keep these questions focused on eliciting more information about what was "good" about the original story. This is not a time to make suggestions.

Figure 10.3: Mathematics inquiry circle protocol.

continued →

Phase 3: Crafting and Claiming a Positive Inquiry Question

This section uses flexible timing; the group agrees on the amount of time necessary for individual reflection and whole-group dialogue.

1. Partners complete a written "storytelling recap" for one another based on the storytelling process and the questions that emerged from the group discussion. Once the partners complete their recap, they give it to the storyteller.
   ♦ Each person reviews his or her notes from the storytelling experience and records responses on the recap sheet. The recap is helpful in creating a shared set of data from the storytelling process and provides written documentation for the storyteller to use as a resource in crafting positive inquiry questions.
2. Partners give storytellers their recap sheet. Students pause and personally reflect on what has been shared as well as what is recorded on the recap sheet. Students should use this time to consider how their personal experience can serve as a beginning point for crafting an inquiry question that builds on some aspect of their reasoning and thinking that is good and strong.
3. Students craft a question for themselves, such as the following, and write it in the center of a sheet of chart paper (on the wall or table) or online in a collaborative document.
   ♦ What really matters when solving mathematics problems?
   ♦ What do you want to carry with you in your problem-solving toolkit?
   ♦ What do you want to change?
4. Students move from chart to chart and silently participate in a written conversation around each proposed question (see the Chalk Talk strategy in chapter 6, page 68). This activity provides an opportunity for students to discuss the proposed questions, exploring and expanding the possibilities of the inquiry. The intent is not to answer or propose ways to resolve questions, but rather to explore related assumptions and ideas. At the conclusion of the chalk talk, each person has time to revise his or her question. The step ends with a go-round in which each person simply states his or her question for beginning an inquiry. It is understood that this question may go through several revisions once the inquiry is in process.
   ♦ For a group rather than individual inquiry, during this step, the teacher reconvenes everyone in one whole-group inquiry circle. Each person writes the themes his or her partner identified from his or her story on chart paper for the group to see. The teacher encourages the group to review the posted themes and discuss using the following prompts.
     • Are there any additional themes or core values that need to be posted?
     • Are any of these themes or core values related?
     • Are any more important than others?
     • Are any less important than another?
     • Will any have greater or lesser impact on our work together?
     • How can we carry forward what we value most?
     • How can powerful work of the past inspire and support present needs to inquire?

Source: Adapted from Bisplinghoff, 2017.

*Visit **go.SolutionTree.com/instruction** for a free reproducible version of this figure.*

This protocol empowers students to take control of their own learning through storytelling, reflection, and inquiry. It builds skills in critical thinking and metacognition as well as communicating to students the high value teachers place on learning and sets the tone for classroom expectations, especially for reluctant learners because it gives a context for why students are learning this concept through a deeper investigation. It also helps build listening and questioning skills for younger students early on. Additionally, for younger students, teachers might want to ask them to reflect via drawing pictures (instead of writing) and shorten the length of discussion.

Figure 10.5 depicts the self-reflection scale for this element so teachers can gauge their performance.

Inquiry Circle Recap Sheet
1. What were the most compelling features of the story?
2. What was the most quotable quote that came out of this storytelling?
3. What was the most significant moment in the storytelling for you as a listener?
4. Did a particularly intriguing, innovative idea emerge during the telling of this story? If so, describe what you learned about it.
5. What three themes or core values stood out for you (how the other student expressed his or her thoughts, used a strategy you haven't thought of, and so on) in the story you heard?
6. What possible inquiry questions did you hear in the story?
7. Use positive language as you attempt to craft possible inquiry questions in support of your partner's work.

Source: Adapted from Bisplinghoff, 2017.

Figure 10.4: Mathematics inquiry circle recap sheet.

*Visit **go.SolutionTree.com/instruction** for a free reproducible version of this figure.*

Score	Description
4: Innovating	I adapt behaviors and create new strategies for unique student needs and situations.
3: Applying	I ask questions of reluctant learners with the same frequency and depth as with high-expectancy students, and I monitor the quality of participation of reluctant learners.
2: Developing	I ask questions of reluctant learners with the same frequency and depth as with high-expectancy students, but I do not monitor the effect on students.
1: Beginning	I use the strategies and behaviors associated with this element incorrectly or with parts missing.
0: Not Using	I am unaware of strategies and behaviors associated with this element.

Figure 10.5: Self-rating scale for element 42—Asking in-depth questions of reluctant learners.

Element 43: Probing Incorrect Answers With Reluctant Learners

When a student responds incorrectly to a question, the teacher can probe the student's answer to guide him or her in revising it until it is correct. Relative to mathematics, a simple way that teachers can do this is through an answer revision process. The theme throughout this book has been a focus on high-level thinking, reasoning, and problem solving. Allowing student to go back and revise based on teacher feedback further encourages students to think about how they originally solved the problem versus how they will now reason through a problem based on new feedback.

In the revision protocol in figure 10.6, the teacher reviews student work (individually as or in a collaborative teacher team). The teacher then provides feedback using a four-quadrant template. The top left quadrant is for strengths, the top right is for areas to review and revise, the bottom left is for recommendations, and the bottom right is for resources that might be useful to the student. It's important that the teacher provides feedback not only on the accuracy and precision of the solution, but on the mathematical thinking the student has shown or not shown in the work. Additionally, recommendations could be in the form of questions to prompt students or support them if they're stuck. Feedback is not about giving students the steps or the right answer, as that defeats the whole revision process.

Strengths:	Areas to review and revise:
Recommendations:	Resources:

Figure 10.6: Revision protocol.

*Visit **go.SolutionTree.com/instruction** for a free reproducible version of this figure.*

Figure 10.7 depicts the self-reflection scale for element 43, probing incorrect answers with reluctant learners, so teachers can gauge their performance.

Score	Description
4: Innovating	I adapt behaviors and create new strategies for unique student needs and situations.
3: Applying	I probe incorrect answers with reluctant learners in the same manner as with high-expectancy students, and I monitor the level and quality of responses of reluctant learners.
2: Developing	I probe incorrect answers with reluctant learners in the same manner as with high-expectancy students, but I do not monitor the effect on students.
1: Beginning	I use the strategies and behaviors associated with this element incorrectly or with parts missing.
0: Not Using	I am unaware of strategies and behaviors associated with this element.

Figure 10.7: Self-rating scale for element 43—Probing incorrect answers with reluctant learners.

GUIDING QUESTIONS FOR CURRICULUM DESIGN

The design question in this chapter focuses on communicating high expectations to all students, especially reluctant learners: *What strategies will I use to help typically reluctant students feel valued and comfortable interacting with me and their peers?* The following questions, which align to each of the elements in this chapter, guide teachers as they plan to communicate high expectations.

- **Element 41:** What will I do to demonstrate value and respect for reluctant learners?

_____

_____

_____

_____

_____

_____

_____

_____

- **Element 42:** What strategies will I use to ask in-depth questions of reluctant learners?

_____

_____

_____

_____

_____

_____

_____

_____

- **Element 43:** How will I probe incorrect answers with reluctant learners?

_____

_____

_____

_____

_____

_____

_____

_____

Summary

Communicating high expectations involves three elements: (1) demonstrating value and respect for reluctant learners, (2) asking in-depth questions of reluctant learners, and (3) probing incorrect answers with reluctant learners. In the mathematics classroom, the expectations a teacher expresses toward a student can have a significant impact on his or her mathematics-related identities.

CHAPTER 11

Developing Expertise

One of the most powerful aspects of *The New Art and Science of Teaching* framework is its granularity. Simply put, this means that the framework describes effective teaching in such detail that educators can pinpoint areas of strength and weakness, set goals to improve in specific areas, select strategies to implement as they seek to improve, track progress as they go, and make subsequent plans for future growth. In this book, we have specifically applied thirty-five of the forty-three elements of *The New Art and Science of Teaching* framework to the mathematics classroom. Thus, a mathematics teacher can use the guidance from chapters 1 through 11, along with a reflective process, to enhance their professional practice.

For example, a mathematics teacher might identify engagement (the seventh design area) as an area of potential improvement for his or her practice. On closer inspection, this teacher might decide to start working on the third element of engagement, using physical movement. Chapter 7 details mathematics-specific strategies that this teacher could implement. The teacher decides to focus on encouraging students to move around to various mathematics stations that ask them to solve problems in different areas of the classroom. However, the teacher realizes he neglected to provide guidance and monitoring on behavior expectations during movement. He corrects his error on subsequent attempts and tracks his progress until he is able to clearly explain and give examples of how the strategy is resulting in increased attention and energy among students. He decides to focus on strategies related to using friendly controversy (particularly textual criticism) next.

This reflective process involves four steps.

1. Conduct a self-audit.
2. Select goal elements and specific strategies.
3. Engage in deliberate practice and track progress.
4. Seek continuous improvement by planning for future growth.

Here we provide details and resources for each step.

Step 1: Conduct a Self-Audit

The reflective process commences with a *self-audit*. Using a developmental scale such as the one we show in figure 12.1 (and found throughout this book as a part of each element), teachers rate themselves on the forty-three elements of *The New Art and Science of Teaching* framework.

Score	Description
4: Innovating	I adapt behaviors and create new strategies for unique student needs and situations.
3: Applying	I use the strategies and behaviors associated with this element, and I monitor the extent to which my actions affect students' performance.
2: Developing	I use the strategies and behaviors associated with this element, but I do not monitor the effect on students.
1: Beginning	I use the strategies and behaviors associated with this element incorrectly or with parts missing.
0: Not Using	I am unaware of strategies and behaviors associated with this element.

Source: Marzano, 2017, p. 104.

Figure 12.1: Developmental scale for elements.

Teachers can use the self-audit form in figure 12.2 to record the results of the self-audit.

Element	4	3	2	1	0
1. Providing scales and rubrics					
2. Tracking student progress					
3. Celebrating success					
4. Using informal assessments of the whole class					
5. Using formal assessments of individual students					
6. Chunking content					
7. Processing content					
8. Recording and representing content					
9. Using structured practice sessions					
10. Examining similarities and differences					
11. Examining errors in reasoning					
12. Engaging students in cognitively complex tasks					
13. Providing resources and guidance					
14. Generating and defending claims					
15. Previewing					
16. Highlighting critical information					
17. Reviewing content					
18. Revising knowledge					
19. Reflecting on learning					
20. Assigning purposeful homework					
21. Elaborating on information					
22. Organizing students to interact					

Element	4	3	2	1	0
23. Noticing and reacting when students are not engaged					
24. Increasing response rates					
25. Using physical movement					
26. Maintaining a lively pace					
27. Demonstrating intensity and enthusiasm					
28. Presenting unusual information					
29. Using friendly controversy					
30. Using academic games					
31. Providing opportunities for students to talk about themselves					
32. Motivating and inspiring students					
33. Establishing rules and procedures					
34. Organizing the physical layout of the classroom					
35. Demonstrating withitness					
36. Acknowledging adherence to rules and procedures					
37. Acknowledging lack of adherence to rules and procedures					
38. Using verbal and nonverbal behaviors that indicate affection for students					
39. Understanding students' backgrounds and interests					
40. Displaying objectivity and control					
41. Demonstrating value and respect for reluctant learners					
42. Asking in-depth questions of reluctant learners					
43. Probing incorrect answers with reluctant learners					

Figure 12.2: Self-audit for *The New Art and Science of Teaching* framework.

*Visit **go.SolutionTree.com/instruction** to download a free reproducible version of this figure.*

Once a teacher has completed the self-audit form in figure 12.2, he or she examines the elements in which he or she assigned the lowest ratings. These are candidates to become growth goals.

Step 2: Select Goal Elements and Specific Strategies

We recommend that teachers identify no more than three growth goals to work on during one school year. For example, a teacher might identify one goal area (such as displaying objectivity and control) to work on from August until November, a different goal area (such as motivating and inspiring students) to work on from December until March, and a final goal area (such as reviewing content) to work on during April and May. Once the teacher identifies a goal area, he or she should decide how long to work on that area and what score on the developmental scale he or she would like to achieve by the end of that time period. For example, a teacher might decide to increase her score on displaying objectivity and control from a 1 (beginning) to a 3 (applying) between August and November.

A mathematics teacher who has decided to work on displaying objectivity and control could examine the appropriate section of chapter 9 in this book and determine that she would like to try two strategies: (1) the PAUSE strategy and (2) actively listen and speak by having daily conversations with all students. She decides that to familiarize herself with the beliefs and thinking of her students, she will ask students to write down answers to a few questions about their thinking and learning.

Step 3: Engage in Deliberate Practice and Track Progress

The process of developing expertise in a particular area follows a predictable progression (as figure 12.1, page 116, and the rating scales throughout this book suggest). At the Not Using (0) level, the teacher is simply not using a strategy or behavior. By choosing to try out a strategy, he or she moves to the Beginning (1) level.

It is normal, when beginning to use a strategy, to execute the strategy or behavior incorrectly or with parts missing. In the case of the teacher working on displaying objectivity and control (element 40), she might begin with the intention of using the PAUSE strategy, but fail to first examine and take steps to correct her implicit biases about students that might affect her behavior and ability to display objectivity and control.

The next level, Developing (2), involves correcting errors or filling in missing pieces. The teacher working on displaying objectivity and control, at this stage, might have correctly identified her implicit biases, and she then moves on to use the PAUSE strategy to promote the open exchange of diverse ideas and help disarm her potentially wrong conclusions about students. At the Developing (2) level, a teacher does not yet monitor the effect of the strategy or behavior on students.

Monitoring how one's actions are affecting student performance is the hallmark of the Applying (3) level. The teacher in our example might achieve this level by administering a questionnaire, compiling student answers, and adjusting her interactions with students (and the way she scaffolds their interactions with each other) based on her findings. She notices that students seem more relaxed and comfortable in her classroom and that students who were previously reluctant to engage in discussions are sharing more frequently.

Finally, a teacher who has progressed to the Innovating (4) level is monitoring students so closely that he or she adapts strategies (or creates new ones if necessary) to ensure that all students are performing at high levels, regardless of their unique needs and situations. A tracking chart like the one in figure 12.3 can help a teacher track his or her progress through each level of the scale.

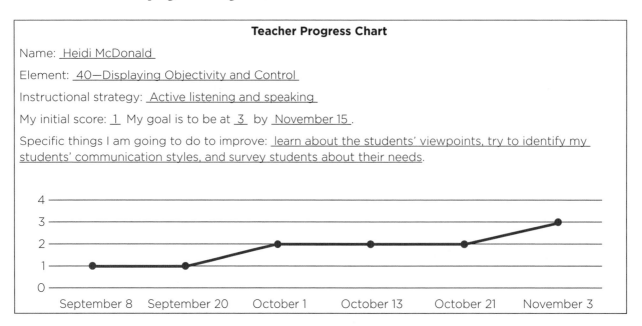

Figure 12.3: Teacher progress for the strategy of understanding cultural backgrounds.

Step 4: Seek Continuous Improvement by Planning for Future Growth

Once a teacher has achieved his or her goal, or the time period he or she set for the completion of the goal has expired, the teacher evaluates his or her current situation and makes plans for the future. For example, the mathematics teacher in the previous example, having achieved her goal for displaying objectivity and control, would move on to her next goal of motivating and inspiring students (element 32).

Summary

The focus of this book is effective instruction in the mathematics classroom. By combining the general model of effective instruction that *The New Art and Science of Teaching* articulates with our mathematics-specific developmental model, we present a comprehensive approach to effective mathematics instruction. Mathematics teachers can use the research and strategies we offer in this book to apply effective instructional strategies in the classroom. The goal of using such instructional strategies is for students to achieve the mental states and processes that decades of research have shown lead to enhanced student learning.

Afterword

The New Art and Science of Teaching (Marzano, 2017) presents a comprehensive model of teaching that organizes all or most of the instructional strategies available to teachers. The science reference is predicated on the fact that these strategies are founded on decades of research and theory and contribute to effective teaching. The art component indicates that factors other than research are attributed to student learning, such as which strategies are used together and how teachers use them for express purposes. This analogy can help elucidate this point:

> Instructional strategies are best likened to techniques an artist might develop and refine over years of practice. The artist then uses these techniques to create works that are not only unique and complex but elegantly focused. The more skill the artist exhibits with available techniques, the better his or her creations. Likewise, the more skill the classroom teacher has with the instructional strategies that research and theory have uncovered over the decades, the better the teacher will be able to create lessons that optimize student learning. (Marzano, 2017, p. 2)

It is the duty, the call to action, and the mission of educators everywhere to meet students where they are and elevate them to the next level of learning. This is an awesome task indeed and extremely rewarding when students move from not knowing to awareness. As teachers endeavor to undertake this responsibility, they need tools, resources, and support to help guide them so they can be the best possible conduit of learning for their charges. *The New Art and Science of Teaching Mathematics* presents myriad strategies to assist teachers in this work. We invite all teachers to raise their own bar of professional capacity so they can, in turn, open the door for the students they are so fortunate to lead.

Appendix A

The New Art and Science of Teaching Framework Overview

As explained in the introduction, *The New Art and Science of Teaching* framework involves three overarching categories—(1) feedback, (2) content, and (3) context. These categories contain the ten design areas, each of which is associated with a specific teacher action, desired student mental states and processes, and a design question to help teachers plan units and lessons within those units. The forty-three individual elements of the model reside within the design areas. Figure A.1 (pages 124–126) presents a comprehensive list of the overarching categories, design areas, teacher actions, desired student mental states and processes, design questions, and elements.

The New Art and Science of Teaching Framework Overview

Category	Design Areas—Teacher Actions	Desired Student Mental States and Processes	Design Questions	Elements
Feedback	1. Providing and Communicating Clear Learning Goals	Students understand the progression of knowledge they are expected to master and where they are along that progression.	How will I communicate clear learning goals that help students understand the progression of knowledge I expect them to master and where they are along that progression?	**1. Providing scales and rubrics** How will I design scales or rubrics? **2. Tracking student progress** How will I track progress? **3. Celebrating success** How will I celebrate success?
	2. Using Assessments	Students understand how test scores and grades relate to their status on the progression of knowledge they are expected to master.	How will I design and administer assessments that help students understand how their test scores and grades relate to their status on the progression of knowledge I expect them to master?	**4. Using informal assessments of the whole class** How will I informally assess the whole class? **5. Using formal assessments of individual students** How will I formally assess individual students?
Content	3. Conducting Direct Instruction Lessons	When content is new, students understand which parts are important and how the parts fit together.	When content is new, how will I design and deliver direct instruction lessons that help students understand which parts are important and how the parts fit together?	**6. Chunking content** How will I chunk the new content into short, digestible bites? **7. Processing content** How will I help students process the individual chunks and the content as a whole? **8. Recording and representing content** How will I help students record and represent their knowledge?
	4. Conducting Practicing and Deepening Lessons	After teachers present new content, students deepen their understanding and develop fluency in skills and processes.	After presenting content, how will I design and deliver lessons that help students deepen their understanding and develop fluency in skills and processes?	**9. Using structured practice sessions** How will I use structured practice? **10. Examining similarities and differences** How will I help students examine similarities and differences? **11. Examining errors in reasoning** How will I help students examine errors in reasoning?

The New Art and Science of Teaching Framework Overview

Category	Design Areas—Teacher Actions	Desired Student Mental States and Processes	Design Questions	Elements
Content	5. Conducting Knowledge Application Lessons	After teachers present new content, students generate and defend claims through knowledge application tasks.	After presenting content, how will I design and deliver lessons that help students generate and defend claims through knowledge application?	**12. Engaging students in cognitively complex tasks** — How will I engage students in cognitively complex tasks? **13. Providing resources and guidance** — How will I provide resources and guidance? **14. Generating and defending claims** — How will I help students generate and defend claims?
	6. Using Strategies That Appear in All Types of Lessons	Students continually integrate new knowledge with old knowledge and revise their understanding accordingly.	Throughout all types of lessons, what strategies will I use to help students continually integrate new knowledge with old knowledge and revise their understanding accordingly?	**15. Previewing strategies** — How will I help students preview content? **16. Highlighting critical information** — How will I highlight critical information? **17. Reviewing content** — How will I help students review content? **18. Revising knowledge** — How will I help students revise knowledge? **19. Reflecting on learning** — How will I help students reflect on their learning? **20. Assigning purposeful homework** — How will I use purposeful homework? **21. Elaborating on information** — How will I help students elaborate on information? **22. Organizing students to interact** — How will I organize students to interact?
Context	7. Using Engagement Strategies	Students are paying attention, energized, intrigued, and inspired.	What engagement strategies will I use to help students pay attention, be intrigued, be energized, and be inspired?	**23. Noticing and reacting when students are not engaged** — What will I do to notice and react when students are not engaged? **24. Increasing response rates** — What will I do to increase students' response rates? **25. Using physical movement** — What will I do to increase students' physical movements? **26. Maintaining a lively pace** — What will I do to maintain a lively pace? **27. Demonstrating intensity and enthusiasm** — What will I do to demonstrate intensity and enthusiasm? **28. Presenting unusual information** — What will I do to present unusual information?

Figure A.1: *The New Art and Science of Teaching* **framework overview.**

continued ↓

The New Art and Science of Teaching Framework Overview

Category	Design Areas—Teacher Actions	Desired Student Mental States and Processes	Design Questions	Elements
Context	7. Using Engagement Strategies	Students are paying attention, energized, intrigued, and inspired.	What engagement strategies will I use to help students pay attention, be energized, be intrigued, and be inspired?	**29. Using friendly controversy** What will I do to engage students in friendly controversy? **30. Using academic games** What will I do to engage students in academic games? **31. Providing opportunities for students to talk about themselves** What will I do to provide opportunities for students to talk about themselves? **32. Motivating and inspiring students** What will I do to motivate and inspire students?
	8. Implementing Rules and Procedures	Students understand and follow rules and procedures.	What strategies will I use to help students understand and follow rules and procedures?	**33. Establishing rules and procedures** What will I do to establish rules and procedures? **34. Organizing the physical layout of the classroom** What will I do to make the physical layout of the classroom most conducive to learning? **35. Demonstrating withitness** What will I do to demonstrate withitness? **36. Acknowledging adherence to rules and procedures** What will I do to acknowledge adherence to rules and procedures? **37. Acknowledging lack of adherence to rules and procedures** What will I do to acknowledge lack of adherence to rules and procedures?
	9. Building Relationships	Students feel welcome, accepted, and valued.	What strategies will I use to help students feel welcome, accepted, and valued?	**38. Using verbal and nonverbal behaviors that indicate affection for students** How will I use verbal and nonverbal behaviors that indicate affection for students? **39. Understanding students' backgrounds and interests** How will I demonstrate that I understand students' backgrounds and interests? **40. Displaying objectivity and control** How will I demonstrate objectivity and control?
	10. Communicating High Expectations	Typically reluctant students feel valued and do not hesitate to interact with the teacher or their peers.	What strategies will I use to help typically reluctant students feel valued and comfortable interacting with their peers or me?	**41. Demonstrating value and respect for reluctant learners** How will I demonstrate value and respect for reluctant learners? **42. Asking in-depth questions of reluctant learners** How will I ask in-depth questions of reluctant learners? **43. Probing incorrect answers with reluctant learners** How will I probe incorrect answers with reluctant learners?

Visit go.SolutionTree.com/instruction for a free reproducible version of this figure.

Appendix B

Lesson Seed: Fluency With the Salute Game

A *lesson seed* is an idea for a specific domain, cluster, or standard that teachers can use to build a lesson. Lesson seeds are not meant to be all-inclusive, nor are they substitutes for instruction, but are activities to help build fluency within a lesson. Figure B.1 outlines the Salute Game protocol (Maryland Department of Education, 2013) using a standard for multiplication and division. The game can be modified for addition, subtraction, and other mathematics skills. Figures B.2 (page 128) and B.3 (page 129) provide directions and materials for the game.

Domain: Operation and Algebraic Thinking Cluster: Represent and Solve Problems Involving Multiplication and Division Standard(s): 3.OA.A.4 Determine the unknown whole number in a multiplication or division equation relating three whole numbers. For example, determine the unknown number that makes the equation true in each of the equations $8 \times ? = 48$, $5 = ? \div 3$, $6 \times 6 = ?$.
Purpose/Big Idea: Students will be able to identify an unknown factor in a multiplication/division situation.
Materials: • Paper or journal and pencil • Directions and 1–10 cards
Activity: The Salute Game • Distribute the directions for salute and two sets of the 1–10 cards to each group of three students. • Model the game with two volunteers from the class. • Allow time for students to play the game. • Students should record the equation they had to solve on a separate sheet of paper or in their mathematics journals. • During that time, move around the room observing the students and determining their ability to use their multiplication facts in the game.

Figure B.1: Solute Game protocol.

continued →

Guiding Questions:

- How did you determine the unknown?

- What property are you using?

- What strategies did use to find the product?

- Why is your answer correct? (Prove it.)

- Does your written equation match the problem or the solution?

- What are the four equations for that fact family?

Source: Maryland Department of Education, 2013.

Source for standard: National Governors Association Center for Best Practices & Council of Chief State School Officers, 2010.

*Visit **go.SolutionTree.com/instruction** for a free reproducible version of this figure.*

Directions for Salute Game (Multiplication Version)

Number of players: Three

Materials: Deck of playing cards (two sets of 0–10 cards, shuffled)

Directions:

1. Players one and two each hold a card to their forehead so that they cannot see it, but the third player can see it.
2. Player three calls out the product.
3. Players one and two race to figure out the numbers on their hidden card.
4. The first player to call out the correct answer is the winner of that round and keeps both cards.
5. The game ends when all the cards have been used. The player with the most cards at the end of the game is the winner.
6. Players should switch roles so that all players get a chance to call out the product.

This game can be modified to practice addition, subtraction, and division facts.

Figure B.2: Solute directions.

*Visit **go.SolutionTree.com/instruction** for a free reproducible version of this figure.*

1–10 Cards for the Salute Game

Make two copies for each group of three students.

1	2	3	4	5
6	7	8	9	10

Figure B.3: Salute cards.

*Visit **go.SolutionTree.com/instruction** for a free reproducible version of this figure.*

Appendix C
List of Figures and Tables

Visit **go.SolutionTree.com/instruction** for free reproducible versions of the figures and tables with an asterisk.

References and Resources

Achieve the Core. (n.d.). *Grades K–8 focus documents*. Accessed at https://achievethecore.org/content/upload/SAP%20Focus%20Math%20K%E2%80%938%2011.12.14.pdf on February 12, 2019.

Berger, W. (2014). *A more beautiful question. The power of inquiry to spark breakthrough ideas*. New York: Bloomsbury.

Bisplinghoff, B. (2017). *Inquiry circles: A protocol for professional inquiry*. Accessed at www.nsrfharmony.org/wp-content/uploads/2017/10/inquiry_circles.pdf on August 3, 2018.

Boaler, J. (2002). Learning from teaching: Exploring the relationship between reform curriculum and equity. *Journal for Research in Mathematics Education, 33*(4), 239–258.

Boaler, J. (2015). *What's math got to do with it? How teachers and parents can transform mathematics learning and inspire success*. New York: Penguin.

Boaler, J. (2016). *Mathematical mindsets: Unleashing students' potential through creative math, inspiring messages and innovative teaching*. San Francisco, CA: Jossey-Bass.

Burns, M. (2004). Ten big math ideas. *Instructor, 113*(7), 16–19.

Center for Academic, Social, and Emotional Learning. (2018). Accessed at www.casel.org on December 19, 2018.

Chappuis, S., & Stiggins, R. J. (2002). Classroom assessment for learning. *Educational Leadership, 60*(1), 40–44.

Danielson, C. (2007). *Enhancing professional practice: A framework for teaching*. Alexandria, VA: Association for Supervision and Curriculum Development.

Dine, F., Evans, P., & Thompson-Grove, G. (2017). *Consultancy*. Accessed at https://www.schoolreforminitiative.org/download/consultancy/ on December 19, 2018.

Dweck, C. S. (2007). *Mindset: The new psychology of success*. New York: Penguin.

Elmore, R. F. (Ed.). (2011). *I used to think . . . and now I think . . . : Twenty leading educators reflect on the work of school reform*. Cambridge, MA: Harvard Education Press.

Fosnot, C. T., & Dolk, M. (2001). *Young mathematicians at work: Constructing multiplication and division*. Portsmouth, NH: Heinemann.

Frey, N., & Fisher, D. (2011). *The formative assessment action plan: Practical steps to more successful teaching and learning.* Alexandria, VA: Association for Supervision and Curriculum Development.

Gino, F. (2018, May 11). *How small acts of thoughtful rebellion can increase your power and status.* Accessed at www.linkedin.com/pulse/how-small-acts-thoughtful-rebellion-can-increase-your-francesca-gino/ on August 3, 2018.

Grant, A. (2016). How to build a culture of originality. *Harvard Business Review, 94*(3), 86–94.

Grant, A. (Producer). (2018, May 10). *WorkLife* [Audio podcast]. Accessed at https://itunes.apple.com/us/podcast/worklife-with-adam-grant/id1346314086?mt=2# on August 3, 2018.

International Center for Leadership in Education. (2018). The Rigor Relevance Framework™. Accessed at http://leadered.com/our-philosophy/rigor-relevance-framework.php on December 19, 2018.

Itzchakov, G., & Kluger, A. N. (2018, May 17). *The power of listening in helping people change.* Accessed at https://hbr.org/2018/05/the-power-of-listening-in-helping-people-change on August 3, 2018.

Jensen, C., Whitehouse, T., & Coulehan, R. (2000, April). Engaging children in the work of mathematicians. *Teaching Children Mathematics, 6*(8), 490–495.

Kanold, T. D., & Larson, M. R. (2015). *Common Core mathematics in a PLC at Work™, leader's guide.* Bloomington, IN: Solution Tree Press.

Kanold, T. D., Schuhl, S., Larson, M. R., Barnes, B., Kanold-McIntyre, J., & Toncheff, M. (2018). *Mathematics assessment and intervention in a PLC at Work™.* Bloomington, IN: Solution Tree Press.

Kirwan, J. V., & Tobias, J. M. (2014). Multiple representations and connections with the Sierpinski triangle. *Mathematics Teacher, 107*(9), 666–671.

Ladd, G.W., Birch, S.H., & Buhs, E.S. (1999). *Children's social and scholastic lives in kindergarten. Related spheres of influence?* Boston: Allyn & Bacon

Lang-Raad, N. (2018). *Everyday instructional coaching.* Bloomington IN: Solution Tree Press

Maryland Department of Education. (2013). *Gr. 3 unit: Represent & solve problems involving multiplication and division.* Accessed at http://mdk12.msde.maryland.gov/instruction/curriculum/mathematics/units/gr3_represent_solve_problems_involving_multiplication_and_division on January 18, 2019.

Marzano, R. J. (2006). *Classroom assessment and grading that work.* Alexandria, VA: Association for Supervision and Curriculum Development.

Marzano, R. J. (2007). *The art and science of teaching.* Alexandria, VA: Association for Supervision and Curriculum Development.

Marzano, R. J. (2012). *The many uses of exit slips.* Accessed at www.ascd.org/publications/educational-leadership/oct12/vol70/num02/The-Many-Uses-of-Exit-Slips.aspx on August 3, 2018.

Marzano, R. (2017). *The new art and science of teaching.* Bloomington, IN: Solution Tree Press.

Marzano, R. J., Marzano, J. S., & Pickering, D. J. (2003). *Classroom management that works: Research-based strategies for every teacher.* Alexandria, VA: Association for Supervision and Curriculum Development.

Marzano, R. J., Pickering, D. J., & Pollock, J. E. (2001). *Classroom instruction that works: Research-based* strategies *for increasing student achievement.* Alexandria, VA: Association for Supervision and Curriculum Development.

McCrea, S. M., Liberman, N., Trope, Y., & Sherman, S. J. (2008). Construal level and procrastination. *Psychological Science, 19*(12), 1308–1314.

McIntosh, M. E. (1997). Communicating mathematically. *The Clearing House, 71*(1), 9–52.

Moschkovich, J. (2012, January). *Mathematics, the Common Core, and language: Recommendations for mathematics instruction for ELs aligned with the Common Core.* Accessed at http://ell.stanford.edu/sites/default/files/pdf/academic-papers/02-JMoschkovich%20Math%20FINAL_bound%20with%20appendix.pdf on August 3, 2018.

Moser, J. S., Schroder, H. S., Heeter, C., Moran, T. P., & Lee, Y.-H. (2011). Mind your errors: Evidence for a neural mechanism linking growth mindset to adaptive post-error adjustments. *Psychological Science, 22,* 1484–1489.

National Council of Teachers of Mathematics. (2000). *Principles and standards for school mathematics.* Reston, VA: Author.

National Governors Association Center for Best Practices & Council of Chief State School Officers. (2010). *Common Core State Standards for mathematics.* Washington, DC: Authors. Accessed at www.corestandards.org/assets/CCSSI_Math%20Standards.pdf on August 6, 2018.

National Governors Association Center for Best Practices & Council of Chief State School Officers. (2013). *High school publishers criteria for the Common Core State Standards for Mathematics.* Accessed at www.corestandards.org/assets/Math_Publishers_Criteria_HS_Spring%202013_FINAL.pdf on February 12, 2019.

National School Reform Faculty. (2015). *Argument-talk protocol.* Accessed at https://nsrfharmony.org/protocols on December 18, 2018.

Nemirovsky, R., Rasmussen, C., Sweeney, G., & Wawro, M. (2012). When the classroom floor becomes the complex plane: Addition and multiplication as ways of bodily navigation. *Journal of the Learning Sciences, 21*(2), 287–323.

Pugalee, D. K. (2001). Writing, mathematics, and metacognition: Looking for connections through students' work in mathematical problem solving. *School Science and Mathematics, 101*(5), 236–245.

Responsive Classroom. (2016). *What is morning meeting?* Accessed on https://www.responsiveclassroom.org/what-is-morning-meeting on December 18, 2018.

Right Question Institute. (n.d.). *What is RTF?* Accessed at https://rightquestion.org/what-is-the-qft on December 18, 2018.

Rimm-Kaufman, S. E., & Yu-Jen, I. (2007). Promoting social and academic competence in the classroom: An intervention study examining the contribution of the responsive classroom approach. *Psychology in the Schools, 44*(4), 397–413.

Rimm-Kaufman, S. E., Larsen, Ross A. A., Baroody, A. E., Curby, T. W., Ko, M., Thomas, J. B., Merritt, E. G., Abry, T., & DeCoster, J. (2014). Efficacy of the Responsive Classroom Approach: Results from a 3-year, longitudinal randomized controlled trial. *American Educational Research Journal, 51*(3), 567–603.

Ritchhart, R., Church, M., & Morrison, K. (2011). *Making thinking visible: How to promote engagement, understanding, and independence for all learners.* San Francisco: Jossey-Bass.

Ritchhart, R., Turner, T., & Hadar, L. (2009). Uncovering students' thinking about thinking using concept maps. *Metacognition and Learning, 4*(2), 145–159.

Rogers C. R., & Roethlisberger, J. (2014, August 1). *Barriers and gateways to communication.* Accessed at https://hbr.org/1991/11/barriers-and-gateways-to-communication on August 3, 2018.

Ross, H. J. (2014). *Everyday bias: Identifying and navigating unconscious judgments in our daily lives.* Lanham, MD: Rowman & Littlefield.

Rothstein, D., Santana, L. (2011). *Make just one change: Teach students to ask their own questions.* Boston: Harvard Education Press.

Rothstein, D., Santana, L., & Minigan, A. (2015). Making questions flow. *Educational Leadership, 73*(1), 70–75.

Simms, J. A. (2016, August). *The critical concepts (final version: English language arts, mathematics, and science).* Centennial, CO: Marzano Research.

Star, J. R., & Rittle-Johnson, B. (2009). Making algebra work: Instructional strategies that deepen student understanding, within and between representations. *ERS Spectrum, 27*(2), 11–18.

Stiggins, R. J. (2008). *Assessment for learning, the achievement gap, and truly effective schools.* Accessed at www.ets.org/Media/Conferences_and_Events/pdf/stiggins.pdf on August 3, 2018.

Stiggins, R., & Chappuis, J. (2008). Enhancing student learning. *District Administration, 44*(1): 42–44.

Stolk, K. (2013). *Types of questions that comprise a teacher's questioning discourse in a conceptually-oriented classroom.* Accessed at https://scholarsarchive.byu.edu/cgi/viewcontent.cgi?article=4715&context=etd on August 3, 2018.

Superkar, K, Swigart, A. G., Tenison, C., Jolles, D., Rosenberg-Lee, M., Fuchs, L., & Menon, V. (2013). Neural predictors of individual differences in response to math tutoring in primary-grade school children. *Proceedings of the National Academy of Sciences of the United States of America, 110*(20):8230–8235.

Tripathi, P. (2008). Developing mathematical understanding through multiple representations. *Mathematics Teaching in the Middle School, 13*(8), 438–445.

University of Copenhagen Faculty. (2017). Math learned best when children move. *ScienceDaily.* Accessed at www.sciencedaily.com/releases/2017/02/170208111619.htm on November 27.

Index